MAR 1 2 2005 **DATE DUE**

MAR 2 6 2005			

DEMCO 38-296

GLOBAL WARMING

By Ron Fridell

Franklin Watts
A Division of Scholastic Inc.
New York Toronto London Auckland Sydney
Mexico City New Delhi Hong Kong
Danbury, Connecticut

Photographs © 2002: Corbis Images: 55 (James L. Amos), 65 (Yann Arthus-Bertrand), 59 (George D. Lepp), 89 (Robert Maass), cover bottom left (David Muench), 17 (Roger Ressmeyer), 105 (Eriko Sugita/Reuters NewMedia Inc.), 81 (Kennan Ward), 15 (Robert Weight/Ecoscene), cover top right (Jeremy Woodhouse); Corbis Sygma/Anthony Fioranelli: 103; European Space Agency: 45; Michigan Technological University, University Relations: 20, 21; MIT News Office/Donna Coveney: 72; NOAA cover bottom right, 16, 42, 43 (Central Library), 14 (NGDC/World Data Center), 49 (L. Stratton/Pacific Marine Environmental Laboratory/TAO Project); Oak Ridge National Laboratory: 27 Peter Arnold Inc./Gordon Wiltsie: 54; Photo Researchers, NY: 29, 92 (Georg Gerster), 52 (Hank Morgan), 62 (Tom Van Sant/Geosphere Project, Santa Monica/SPL), 60 (D.P. Wilson), 61 (Art Wolfe); Reprinted by permission from Nature 405:425-429 (2000), copyright Macmillan Publishers Ltd./Raul Cunha and Pat Smith, Department of Physics, University of Toronto: 12; Scripps Institution of Oceanography Library, University of California, San Diego: 56 (Keeling and Whorf), 32; USDA/Agricultural Research Service: 85; Visuals Unlimited/Bernd Wittich: 92 inset; www.ArtToday.com: cover top left.

Library of Congress Cataloging-in-Publication Data

Fridell, Ron.
    Global Warming / by Ronald Fridell
        p. cm.
    Includes bibliographical references and index.
    Summary: Describes several different theories on the causes and solutions of global warming, including a brief history of Earth's temperature ranges, scientists' predictions for the future, and governments' reactions.
    ISBN 0-531-11900-9
        1. Global warming—Juvenile literature. [1. Global warming. 2. Climatic changes. 3. Climatology.] I. Title.

QC981.8.G56 F75 2002
363.738'74—dc21
                                                                              2001024886

2 3 4 5 6 7 8 9 10 R 11 10 09 08 07 06 05 04 03

Contents

Acknowledgments

I would like to thank my editors, Melissa Stewart and Melissa Palestro, for carefully shepherding the book through its many stages, from concept to final product. I would also like to thank Janann V. Jenner, Ph.D., for reviewing the manuscript and providing insightful suggestions for improvement. Finally, I would like to thank Patricia Walsh, my wife and comrade-in-writing, for helping me to keep the book moving in the right direction.

Good News & Bad News

Picture yourself stepping into a time machine and stepping out at the end of the twenty-first century. What kind of world do you find?

Climate scientists are hard at work trying to formulate a picture of that future world. Wildlife biologists, economists, chemists, engineers, and computer scientists are working with them. Most of these experts agree that the world of A.D. 2100 will be warmer than the world today. Evidence shows that global temperatures have increased an average of 0.9° Fahrenheit (0.5° Celsius) in the last two hundred years, with half of that rise coming about since 1970. This *global warming* trend is unprecedented in recent history, say experts, and it probably will continue.

But while these experts agree that the planet is warming, they do not agree on why it is doing so or on how much warmer it will get. They also disagree on the possible consequences of a warmer Earth. When climate experts look into the planet's future, some see the good news of global warming and some see the bad.

First, here is the good news for humanity that some of these experts foresee: Stepping from your time machine into the world of 2100, you see that you have landed at Chicago's lakefront and are looking out on Lake Michigan. You are facing east with your back to the city. The first thing that strikes you is how green the trees and grass are—a deep, lush green. The next thing you notice is how clean and crisp the air is—and how quiet. Instead of the familiar roar of traffic, all you hear is a gentle hum. When you turn to face the city, you see the reason why. The sleek vehicles gliding along the highway are powered by clean, quiet-running *fuel cells* and electric batteries.

Later, you learn that all of the *fossil fuels* that supplied energy a hundred years ago have been replaced by clean, *renewable energy sources*, such as wind and solar power. You also learn that while the world's overall climate is warmer than it was a hundred years ago, most of this warming has come in the mid-latitudes of the Northern Hemisphere, where it has come as a welcome change. While the planet's population has doubled during the century, from 6 billion to 12 billion, most nations are better off economically than they were at the century's start. Some nations experience temporary flooding or drought problems from time to time, especially *developing nations*, such as India and Brazil, whose rapidly increasing populations are still heavily dependent on agriculture. But these nations have prepared for lean periods by taking advantage of nutritious new strains of plant seeds to increase crop production and by stockpiling emergency supplies of rice, wheat, and other vital food sources.

All these positive changes over the last hundred years have come about because of global warming. This global warming has changed the natural state of the planet for the better.

Now here is the bad news that other climate experts foresee: as you step from your time machine into the year 2100, Chicago's lakefront looks, smells, and sounds very different. The air is hazy and sour with pollution, and the traffic roars along the highway behind you. Things even feel different—the grass beneath your feet feels squishy. You see that a seawall has been built along the lakefront and that waves are lapping up over the top of it. Later, you learn that sea levels have risen dramatically worldwide. Most beaches along the Atlantic Coast, from Maine to Florida, have disappeared, and the islands that make up the Florida Keys are underwater, as are large sections of New York City, Boston, Baltimore, and Miami.

The United States and other wealthy nations have built seawalls like the one in Chicago to help control some of the flooding (for now, at least). Things are very different in developing nations, such as Bangladesh and Indonesia, which don't have the money and technology to control the damage. Floods brought on by a catastrophic combination of rising sea levels and extreme storms have turned these nations into swamps, leaving tens of millions of people dead or homeless.

Other developing nations, whose populations depend on agriculture for survival, have suffered prolonged droughts, particularly the nations of sub-Saharan Africa. With nothing to eat and nowhere to turn, tens of millions of these drought victims, along with the tens of millions of flood victims, roam Earth as *environmental refugees*.

Still other nations have seen their climate turn dramatically cold. Ireland now has the climate of the Arctic Circle. Much of northern Europe is uninhabitable because of cold and floods. No part of the planet is untouched.

All these negative changes over the last hundred years have come about because of global warming. This global warming has changed the natural state of the planet for the worse.

Neither of these pictures of the future is likely to come true. These good news–bad news projections represent the extremes of what climate experts foresee. They are the best things that could possibly happen as well as the worst. They also show just how widely climate experts disagree on the possible impacts of global warming.

This controversy includes the debate over what or who is responsible for recent global warming. A majority of climate experts lays the responsibility squarely on human beings. However, a small but significant minority of climate experts disagree. These experts insist that people are not responsible for these changes. They insist that this warming is entirely natural and that we have no reason to worry about its effects on Earth's climate.

Meanwhile, climate scientists research global warming from every possible angle. What impacts will it have on the life of the planet, they ask, and how can we deal with these impacts? This book examines this global warming controversy and explores the urgent search for answers.

Chapter 1

A Sudden Warming

This search for answers to the nature of global warming begins with evidence from billions of years ago, when Earth's current climate was just beginning to develop. To understand the climate's distant past, we first need to clarify the difference between climate and weather.

Weather is the short-term, day-to-day changes in the atmosphere. These changes include the shifts in temperature, precipitation, and wind and cloud conditions that make up daily weather forecasts. Weather changes on a daily basis.

Climate, on the other hand, changes only over long periods of time. Climate is the average pattern of weather over decades and centuries. It is influenced by slow changes in the ocean, the land, Earth's orbit around the Sun, and the Sun's energy output. Climate remains more or less constant during a person's lifetime but changes through the centuries.

Climate's Ups and Downs

Earth's climate has continued to change over its roughly 4.5-billion-year history, cycling through various warm and cool periods. How cool has Earth's climate gotten? Climate scientists estimate that, roughly 2.4 billion years ago, average global

Illustration of the "Snowball Earth" concept.

temperatures ranged as low as −90° F (−68° C). Glaciers reached all the way from the North and South Poles to the equator, and oceans were covered with sheets of ice. Climate scientists call this phenomenon "Snowball Earth."

How warm has Earth's climate gotten? Roughly 100 million years ago global temperatures averaged 10 to 20° F (5.5 to 11° C) higher than temperatures today. Dinosaurs lived as far north as the Arctic Circle and palm trees grew in the area that is now Chicago.

For most of Earth's history, *ice ages* have alternated with ice-free *interglacial periods*. For roughly the last 100 million years, they have alternated in a 100,000-year pattern that has looked something like this:

- It starts with an 80,000-year period during which ice builds up and glaciers extend from the poles toward the equator.
- It is followed by a 10,000-year period during which ice remains at maximum level.
- This is followed by another 10,000-year period during which ice melts and glaciers retreat back toward the poles.
- Then the pattern repeats itself.

The last ice age ended about 12,500 years ago. At present the planet is in the midst of an interglacial period known as the Holocene. Global climate within an interglacial period routinely cycles through mini-cold and mini-warm periods that may last for thousands of years. Within the last two hundred years, Earth's global temperature has risen very sharply.

Some climate experts believe that this sudden warming is an unnatural and dangerous trend. Others say that it's perfectly natural and not dangerous at all. Is this latest global warming trend something to worry about? Why is it happening? And if it continues, what impacts will it have on the environment and on human society?

The Milankovitch Effect

Climate scientists have a theory to explain why the planet's climate cycles through ice ages and interglacial periods. This theory concerns changes in the distribution of solar energy as Earth orbits the Sun.

Since Earth is a sphere, solar energy from incoming sunlight is not distributed evenly. The angle of incoming sunlight is always more direct in the tropics, the region at and near the equator, than it is anywhere else on the planet. So the tropics receive more incoming solar energy than do the poles.

Earth's orbit, tilt, and proximity to the Sun change on a

Milutin Milankovich.

regular basis over thousands of years. Scientists call these changes the Milankovitch Effect, after Milutin Milankovitch, the Serbian mathematician who first explained these changes in the 1930s. Changes from the Milankovitch Effect can result in as much as a 10 percent difference in the amount of sunlight hitting a given spot on Earth. When these changes combine to direct less incoming sunlight to the northern latitudes, the planet is primed for an ice age. When they combine to direct more sunlight to the northern latitudes, the planet is primed for a warmer interglacial period. According to the Milankovitch Effect, Earth should now be in the midst of a long cooling period.

Learning from the Past

Some climate scientists, known as *paleoclimatologists*, search for answers by looking deep into Earth's past. Paleoclimatologists want to know whether anything like this amount of global warming—0.9° F (0.5° C) in two hundred years—has ever happened before. And if it did happen, what caused it and what impacts did it have on Earth's climate? To put it another way, if climate history is repeating itself, then what lessons can we learn from the past?

Climate scientists who deal with the present, known as climatologists, use data collected from thermometers and rain gauges on the surface of Earth, weather balloons in the upper atmosphere, and satellites in outer space. Paleoclimatologists need to gather other types of data, which they call *proxy data*. Proxy data consists of evidence drawn from natural environmental sources such as ice from ice caps and glaciers, sediment from shorelines and ocean bottoms, tree rings, and holes dug deep into the soil. Paleoclimatologists use this proxy data to help them infer what past climates were like and how they got that way.

A man prepares to release a weather balloon at an Antarctic research station.

An artist's rendition of a weather satellite in orbit.

Paleoclimatologists collecting proxy data about Earth have been compared to doctors giving patients physical examinations. First, they look at a subject's surface, poking and prodding. Then, they look beneath the surface with sophisticated instruments. Finally, they send probes inside the subject to collect samples and then analyze the samples in laboratories.

Ice-Core Research

Ice cores are a prime source of proxy data. Scientists collect long, narrow cores of polar ice by driving hollow tubes into the miles-thick ice sheets of Antarctica and Greenland and bringing up the captured materials. Ice in the extracted cores is arranged in horizontal layers of hard-packed snow that has crystallized over time. Summer ice is distinct from winter ice because it's composed of larger crystals with a higher concentration of acid. Experienced scientists can read these layers to get a rough idea of how the climate has changed over the years. Nearly everything that fell in each year's snow remains behind, locked in the polar ice. This includes trapped

Curator Geoffery Hargreaves inspects a core sample from the
Greenland ice sheet. The samples, stored at −33° F (−36° C),
are examined for evidence of global warming caused by rising carbon
dioxide levels.

air bubbles filled with gases that were present in the atmosphere at the time Some of these bubbles hold air that is as much as 20,000 years old. Once an ice core is extracted from an ice cap or glacier, it's flown to a lab for analysis

In the lab, thin slices of ice are sawed off the core and melted in sealed chambers so that the contents of the trapped water and air bubbles can be analyzed. Among other things, scientists have learned that the air the ancient Egyptians breathed was similar to the air we breathe today, minus the addition of air pollutants that come from human activities.

Sediment Research

Sediment is another source of proxy data. Sediment is soil and stones that have been left behind by glaciers or have settled to the bottoms of oceans or lakes or along shorelines.

One sediment study conducted by an international team of researchers found evidence that part of the vast west Antarctic ice sheet might have collapsed during a previous interglacial period. The team determined this by analyzing sediment recovered from beneath the Antarctic ice. In this sediment they found remains of diatoms, which are microscopic, single-celled marine algae with hard shells. From this proxy evidence, researchers infer that some 400,000 years ago, the Antarctic ice cap was an open ocean warm enough to support these warm-water creatures.

Another sediment study conducted at the other end of the world showed similar results. Julie Brigham-Grette, a climate scientist from the University of Massachusetts, analyzed patterns of rocky sediment deposited in rings along ancient beaches in northwestern Alaska. "It's like a bathtub ring around the coastline,"[1] she said. By examining a series of aerial photographs, she could see how the sea level had risen and fallen over time. Her results showed that about 400,000 years ago the sea level was 60 feet (18 meters) higher than it is today.

Together, these two sediment studies suggest that roughly 400,000 years ago, Earth's climate became so warm that the ice caps at both poles melted.

Tree-Ring Research

Climate scientists also find clues to past climates in tree trunks. One research team from Michigan Technical University made a dramatic find when they learned of a mummified forest of ancient spruce trees on Michigan's Upper Peninsula. A professor from the university got word that miners had uncovered a small forest of buried trees in a sand pit. Scientists hurried to the spot and found 5 acres (2 hectares) of perfectly preserved ancient forest, right down to the moss on the bark.

The scientists concluded that about 10,000 years ago, as glaciers were retreating northward, a sudden shift to warmer temperatures melted the ice. The sudden flood of water brought a flood of fine-grained sand with it, which buried the trees and prevented them from rotting.

The forest was about to be destroyed as part of the mining operation. Students and professors worked quickly to drain the water from part of this ancient forest and build earthen dikes to keep it dry. Then they used chain saws to collect 140 crosssections from the mummified trees.

Trees cover themselves entirely with a new layer of wood each year. This layer extends all along the trunk from top to bottom, as well as down into the roots and out into the branches. These new, annual layers show up in the crosssection of a trunk as growth rings. In years where more precipitation than usual falls, the growth rings are thick. In drier years, the rings are thinner. If the climate 10,000 years ago had shown any hint of getting warmer and wetter, the trees in the ancient forest would have shown it in their growth rings—but they didn't. This evidence led the tree-ring research team to conclude that 10,000 years ago, as the

A scientist uses a chain saw to cut a
preserved tree to expose its rings.

In Michigan, scientists and students had to work quickly while the water was held back by dikes and pumps. After the study was complete, the area was reflooded.

glaciers retreated, Earth's climate warmed extremely suddenly and without warning.

Borehole Research

Paleoclimatologists have a unique method of taking Earth's past temperatures. They use holes that were bored into the soil by modern-day people looking for water or minerals. Some of these boreholes reach down as far as 1,800 feet (549 meters). The top few feet of the ground warm up and cool down with the change in seasons. These temperature changes continue rippling down through the soil into the rocks below, to depths of 1,640 feet (500 meters) or more. The deeper these ripples of heat and cold travel, the more slowly they move. Scientists have calculated their speed of movement. These descending ripples of surface warmth and cold take about a hundred years to reach a depth of 492 feet (150 m) and a thousand years to travel 1,640 feet (500 m).

By lowering sensitive thermometers deep into these boreholes and taking measurements every 3.3 feet (10 m), scientists can obtain a record of surface temperatures reaching as far as 1,000 years into the past. "The upper 500 meters [1,640 feet] is an archive," said Professor Henry Pollack of the University of Michigan. "If you drilled a borehole anywhere on a continent, you could observe a temperature profile and be able to reconstruct what had happened at that location."[2]

More than 600 boreholes in North America, Europe, Africa, and Australia have been monitored. Researchers have collected all this temperature data and averaged it, year by year, to obtain a record of Earth's global temperature. The data shows that 80 percent of the sites are hotter today than they were five centuries ago.

What Proxy Data Shows

The results of this borehole research, along with the proxy results from sediment and tree-ring research, indicate that Earth's climate has been gradually cooling over most of the last 100 million years. But a gradual warming trend has set in since the coldest part of the last ice age, 20,000 years ago. Since then, global temperatures have been relatively stable, increasing at an estimated rate of about 1° F (0.6° C) every 3,000 years.

And what about the recent past? By combining their proxy data, paleoclimatologists have been able to extend the temperature record for the Northern Hemisphere back about 1,000 years. They have found that the twentieth century was the warmest century of the last five and that the 1990s were the warmest decade of the entire millennium.

Many other climate scientists agree that the global temperature increase of 0.9° F (0.5° C) in the last two hundred years, with half of that increase occurring since 1970, is unprecedented in recent climate history. Many climate scientists also agree that the cause of this warming is not natural but human-made.

Chapter 2

What Causes Global Warming?

The Natural Greenhouse Effect

The majority of climate scientists suspects that recent global warming can be blamed on a sudden and steadily growing increase in the *greenhouse effect* caused by the burning of fossil fuels. If this increase in the greenhouse effect turns out to be harmful, it will be a matter of too much of a good thing, because the greenhouse effect is a life-giving process. Without the greenhouse effect, our planet would be uninhabitable.

How does the greenhouse effect work? In an actual greenhouse—a building with a glass roof and glass sides that is kept warm for growing plants—glass lets sunlight through. Some of this sunlight is absorbed by the soil and plants inside, but some of it bounces back in the form of *infrared rays*. Without the glass to stop its flight, that infrared energy would leave the greenhouse. Instead, the glass re-reflects it back inside and keeps it there to warm the air inside the greenhouse.

Earth's atmosphere works something like the glass of a greenhouse. About two-thirds of the energy that the Sun pours into Earth's atmosphere is absorbed by the oceans and land. Most of the rest is reflected back out into space. Some of this eflected energy, however, is re-reflected back down to Earth's surface by ases in the atmosphere.

These gases are called *greenhouse gases* because they act somewhat like he glass roof and walls of a greenhouse. They have the power to re-reflect ome of the Sun's infrared energy back down to Earth, where it warms the tmosphere. The average temperature of the Earth's surface is 59° F (15° C). Without greenhouse gases, the average global temperature would plummet to 0° F (−18° C).

These greenhouse gases, which make such a big difference, are only a mall part of Earth's atmosphere. Minus water vapor, the atmosphere is omposed almost exclusively of nitrogen (78 percent) and oxygen (21 per-ent). The remaining 1 percent is primarily argon, with only tiny amounts f other gases, known as trace gases. Greenhouse gases consist of water apor and trace gases.

Water vapor is by far the most abundant greenhouse gas. Along with he other greenhouse gases, water vapor makes the air warmer. But unlike hose other greenhouse gases, the amount of water vapor in the atmosphere s constantly rising and falling. The more the atmosphere warms, the more vater that evaporates from the surface of the planet, which puts more water apor into the air, which creates more warming, which produces more water apor, which creates more warming, and so on.

If this water vapor kept building up and building up, the Earth's tem-erature would keep rising and rising. But as we know, this is not the case. When the water vapor builds up to a certain point, it condenses into clouds nd falls to Earth in the form of cooling rain or snow. This natural heating nd cooling cycle helps keep Earth's temperature steady and the climate abitable. The greenhouse effect keeps the planet warm, but not too warm.

Greenhouse-Gas Buildup

But what would happen if more and more greenhouse gases kept being added to the air and never taken out? What if, instead of condensing and falling back to Earth, these added greenhouse gases remained in the atmosphere and kept building up and building up, carrying the greenhouse effect to extremes?

The atmosphere of the planet Venus shows what happens when the greenhouse effect is taken to extremes. Whereas greenhouse gases make up only a tiny part of Earth's atmosphere, they make up most of the atmosphere of Venus. As a result, the Venusian sky is blanketed with dense clouds composed of a nearly liquid form of the greenhouse gas *carbon dioxide*. These Venusian clouds are so dense that they allow almost no solar energy to enter the planet's atmosphere. But they also allow almost no solar energy to escape. Instead of cycling in and out, as it does on Earth, the solar energy that gets into Venus's atmosphere stays there. As a result, the surface temperature of Venus is hot enough to melt lead, about 900° F (482° C). It is uninhabitable because of an out-of-control greenhouse effect.

Near the beginning of Earth's existence billions of years ago, its atmosphere was similar to Venus's, containing about 95 percent carbon dioxide. Later, as more and more carbon dioxide was absorbed by oceans and plants, the greenhouse effect became less and less extreme, and Earth and its atmosphere gradually cooled.

Recently, though, greenhouse gases have been building up in Earth's atmosphere. Most of this buildup is carbon dioxide, and this buildup has many climate scientists concerned. They believe that more and more carbon dioxide in the atmosphere will lead to more and more global warming

The Carbon Cycle

To understand their concern, it is important to understand how the greenhouse gas carbon dioxide is cycled into and out of the atmosphere. Carbon dioxide is cycled into the air by human beings and other animals. Each time we inhale, we take in oxygen, and each time we exhale, we send out carbon dioxide. Organic matter from dead animals and plants also contributes to atmospheric carbon dioxide. As this organic matter decays, the element *carbon* is released. This carbon recombines with atmospheric oxygen to form carbon dioxide. Green plants add small amounts of carbon dioxide to the air at night through the process known as respiration, but plants quickly reuse this carbon dioxide during photosynthesis.

Photosynthesis is the process through which green plants cycle carbon dioxide out of the atmosphere. During photosynthesis, plants absorb carbon dioxide and break it down into carbon and oxygen. The carbon then

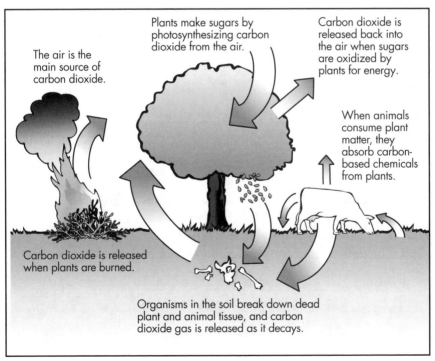

The air is the main source of carbon dioxide.

Plants make sugars by photosynthesizing carbon dioxide from the air.

Carbon dioxide is released back into the air when sugars are oxidized by plants for energy.

When animals consume plant matter, they absorb carbon-based chemicals from plants.

Carbon dioxide is released when plants are burned.

Organisms in the soil break down dead plant and animal tissue, and carbon dioxide gas is released as it decays.

The Carbon Cycle

recombines with other chemicals inside the plants to form the sugars and starches that plants use to live and grow.

Oceans and land also cycle carbon dioxide out of the atmosphere. Electrically charged atoms in Earth's oceans absorb so much carbon dioxide that scientists refer to oceans as *carbon sinks*. Land is another carbon sink. Plants and animals that get buried in soil before they decay aboveground take their carbon underground with them.

Early in Earth's history, when the atmosphere was 95 percent carbon dioxide, green plants began growing, first in the ocean and then on land. As more of these plants grew, more carbon dioxide was removed from the atmosphere through photosynthesis. And as more of these plants died and were buried in the soil and at sea, more carbon was stored underground and kept out of the atmosphere.

Some of this carbon buried on land turned first into peat, then lignite, then coal. Some of it turned into oil and natural gas. Together, coal, oil, and natural gas are known as fossil fuels because they come from the remains of ancient organisms.

All these events took place well before human beings came along. By the time they did, an estimated 5 trillion tons (4.5 trillion metric tons) of carbon had accumulated within the soil in the form of fossil fuels. With all this carbon being taken out of the atmosphere, the percentage of atmospheric carbon dioxide had been steadily dropping over Earth's 4.5-billion-year history, from 95 percent to less than 0.3 percent. That 0.3 percent concentration has remained constant throughout nearly all of human history. The *carbon cycle* has remained in balance, and the result has been a moderate greenhouse effect that has kept the planet at a habitable temperature.

The Enhanced Greenhouse Effect

This was the case until the nineteenth century. Then the percentage of carbon dioxide in the atmosphere began rising as a result of human activities. The *industrial revolution* began in England, Europe, and the United States in the mid-nineteenth century. Factories sprang up, filled with machines fueled by coal and oil dug up from deep within Earth. Then, around the turn of the twentieth century, automobiles that ran on gasoline, another fossil fuel, began to become an important part of life in *industrialized nations*, such as America and England.

As more and more fossil fuels were taken from Earth and burned for energy, more and more carbon dioxide was released back into the atmosphere. At the same time, as the world's population increased, more and more forests were cleared to make room for agricultural lands and to provide timber for building. The result was the existence of fewer trees to absorb carbon dioxide from the atmosphere through photosynthesis. This

This area in Brazil was cleared for agriculture.

deforestation continues today, with more tropical forest being converted to farmland and cattle ranches every day. In 1999 alone, logging and farming reduced the size of the Amazon rain forests by an area the size of the state of Hawaii.

The result of this burning of fossil fuels and clearing of forests is what climate scientists call the *enhanced greenhouse effect*—enhanced by human activities. With more greenhouse gases in the air reflecting the Sun's infrared rays back down to Earth's surface, Earth's surface temperature seems destined to keep rising.

The Other Greenhouse Gases

The other greenhouse gases, besides water vapor and carbon dioxide, are *methane* (CH_4), *nitrous oxide* (N_2O), *ozone* (O_3), and *chlorofluorocarbons* (CFCs).

- Methane is the second most important greenhouse gas, next to carbon dioxide, that results from human activities. It is sometimes called marsh gas because it bubbles up from marshy areas where organic materials are decomposing. Methane is also released during coal mining, and oil drilling, from the guts of termites and cows, and from decaying material in landfills (see "Recycle Waste" on page 103). Human activities have increased the atmospheric concentration of methane by an estimated 145 percent in the last two hundred years.
- Nitrous oxide is a human anesthetic that is commonly called laughing gas. It is released by various human activities in the chemical industry and in agriculture. Its atmospheric concentration has increased by an estimated 15 percent in the last two hundred years.
- Ozone is produced naturally when ultraviolet radiation from the Sun acts on oxygen molecules. Industrial activities, including the emission of nitrogen oxides from motor vehicles and power plants, enhance ozone production.
- Chlorofluorocarbons are human-made chemicals that, once released into the atmosphere, remain there for up to two hundred years. Thanks to an international treaty, the production of chlorofluorocarbons is being phased out (see "The Montreal Protocol" on page 87).

Besides water vapor, carbon dioxide is the biggest contributor to the enhanced greenhouse effect. It is responsible for an estimated 70 percent of the global temperature increase. Of the other major greenhouse gases, methane contributes about 24 percent and nitrous oxide about 6 percent to the increase. Carbon dioxide still makes up less than 1 percent of the atmosphere, but that percentage is on the rise. Presently, human activities release about 7.7 billion tons (7 billion t) of carbon dioxide into the atmosphere each year, adding to the 827 billion tons (750 billion t) already there. Of this additional 7.7 billion tons (7 billion t), about 3.3 billion tons (3 billion t) are removed by the carbon sinks of plants and oceans. The other 4.4 billion tons (4 billion t) remain in the air and will not go away anytime soon. Scientists estimate that carbon dioxide remains in the atmosphere for up to two hundred years. The result is an atmospheric concentration of carbon dioxide that paleoclimatologists say is higher than it has been at any time during the last 450,000 years.

Electrically charged atoms in ocean waters can absorb only about one-third of this additional carbon dioxide. The rest remains in the atmosphere, enhancing the greenhouse effect. By the end of the twenty-first century, the volume of carbon dioxide released into the atmosphere by human activities is expected to be double or even triple what it was at the start of the century.

If, as many climate scientists believe, the natural carbon cycle cannot handle the additional carbon dioxide released by human activities, the greenhouse effect will keep increasing and Earth's temperature will keep rising until it reaches dangerous levels.

Or will it?

Chapter 3

How Hot Will It Get?

Early Warnings

Alarms about the effects of human-produced carbon dioxide were sounded as early as 1896. That was when Swedish chemist Svante Arrhenius asked, "Is the mean temperature of the ground in any way influenced by the presence of heat-absorbing gases in the atmosphere?"[1]

Arrhenius answered his own question by calculating that doubling the concentration of carbon dioxide would boost global temperatures significantly. Scientists didn't pay much attention to Arrhenius's predictions at the time and they had little to say about global warming for the next sixty years. Then, in 1957, two climate scientists issued an alarming report on a study

Roger Revelle collects samples on the *RV Scripps*.

hey had just completed. Humanity was now "engaged in a great geophysical experiment,"[2] they warned, an experiment we were conducting with Earth and its atmosphere as our laboratory. The world's oceans could no longer absorb the excess carbon dioxide we were releasing into the air, they announced. As a result, we were changing the composition of the planet's atmosphere and forcing nature to change its behavior in ways that we could not possibly foresee.

The scientists were Roger Revelle and Hans Suess of the Scripps Institute of Oceanography in San Diego, California. Revelle and Suess's report captured the attention of the scientific community, and other scientists conducted carbon dioxide research studies that yielded similar results. A landmark 1965 report by the President's Science Advisory Committee warned that, by the year 2000, atmospheric carbon dioxide "may be sufficient to produce measurable and perhaps marked changes in climate, and will almost certainly cause significant changes in temperature and other properties of the stratosphere."[3]

In 1979 a panel of the National Academy of Sciences warned of significant climate changes taking place worldwide. The panel's report warned that "A wait-and-see policy may mean waiting until it is too late."[4]

In the late 1980s James Hansen and other climate scientists from the National Aeronautics and Space Administration (NASA) analyzed surface temperatures from two thousand reporting stations around the world. Though daily temperatures had been recorded at these stations for decades, no one had ever collected and analyzed this data.

In testimony before Al Gore's Senate Committee on Science, Technology, and Space in 1988, Hansen said that this analysis of global temperatures showed that Earth was definitely warming and that the cause was definitely excess carbon dioxide in the atmosphere caused by human activities, which was enhancing the greenhouse effect. Hansen predicted that the 1990s would be warmer and that this warming would continue in the twenty-first century, leading to serious global consequences.

Hansen's remarks were widely quoted in the press. Previous warnings had caught the attention of the scientific community but not the attention of anyone else. Hansen's warning carried the issue beyond the laboratory for the first time. Suddenly, global warming became a serious political issue.

While climate scientists conducted more studies on global warming, government leaders began taking positions on the issue. In 1992 Senator Al Gore published a best-selling book about the subject, *Earth in the Balance*, which treated global warming as a serious threat to Earth's future.

On July 24, 1997, President Bill Clinton held a press conference to announce that a scientific *consensus* had been reached on global warming. He said that climate experts all around the world now agreed that global warming due to an enhanced greenhouse effect produced by excess carbon dioxide from the burning of fossil fuels was a reality. These climate experts also agreed that global warming signaled a coming global catastrophe, Clinton said. These things were facts, he announced, not theories.

In his January 28, 2000, State of the Union address, President Clinton again sounded the alarm: "If we fail to reduce the emission of greenhouse gases," he announced, "deadly heat waves and droughts will become more frequent, coastal areas will flood, and economies will be disrupted. That is going to happen unless we act."[5]

What the Facts Say

But was President Clinton correct? Is there really a scientific consensus on global warming? Does the scientific community really agree that higher concentrations of greenhouse gases will inevitably increase surface temperatures until there is a global catastrophe?

To find out, let's begin by looking at the accepted facts on global surface temperature.

- The surface temperature of the planet has risen about 0.9° F (0.5° C) since the 1800s, with half of that increase occurring since 1970.
- Until 1990, the six warmest years in recorded history all came in the 1980s, with 1988 being the warmest.
- The 1990s were warmer still. Six of those years were warmer than the previous 1988 record, with 1998 being the warmest in history and 1999 the second warmest.

Now let's look at the accepted facts on carbon dioxide emissions.

- Each year we add 4.4 billion tons (4 billion t) of carbon dioxide to the atmosphere, which will remain there for at least the next hundred years.
- Since the 1800s, human activities have contributed to a 20–30 percent increase in atmospheric carbon dioxide, to a level of 360 parts per million (ppm), the highest concentration in the last 420,000 years.
- The primary human activities contributing to this increase of atmospheric carbon dioxide are the burning of fossil fuels and the cutting down of forests, both of which are increasing each year.

Nearly all scientists agree on the above facts. But this is as far as the "scientific consensus" that President Clinton spoke of actually goes. The majority of climate scientists say they believe that increased global warming is linked to increased carbon dioxide emissions due to human activities. We'll call them the believers. But a significant minority of climate scientists have their doubts. We'll call them the dissenters.

What the Believers Say

Some believers are more cautious than others. Climate scientist John Houghton is one of the cautious believers. He says that experts can't say for certain that global warming is caused by human activities but that "we have good reasons for believing that the effect is real."[6]

Houghton is one of the leaders of the Intergovernmental Panel on Climate Change (IPCC) of the United Nations. With a membership of 2,500 climate experts from around the world, the panel is the largest and most influential scientific organization ever to address global climate change. A 1995 IPCC report about human activities states that "the balance of evidence suggests that there is a discernible influence on climate."[7]

The *New York Times* called the panel's findings important because "experts advising the world's governments on climate change are saying for the first time that human activity is a likely cause of the warming of the global atmosphere."[8] Regular IPCC reports issued since then have reaffirmed this view of a direct link between global warming and the burning of fossil fuels.

Other believers are less cautious than Houghton and the IPCC. They don't use words like "suggests" and "likely" when they speak of the connection between human activities and climate change. They are absolutely certain of the connection. Climate scientist James McCarthy states that there is no debate in the scientific community about the fact that global warming is caused by human activities. "The only debate," he says, "is the rate at which it's happening."[9] Climate scientist Michael MacCracken adds that human activities are "dramatically modifying atmospheric composition and this is going to change the climate."[10] And Tom Karl of the National Climate Data Center (NCDC) agrees. "The climate reality is that if you look out your window, part of what you see in terms of the weather is produced by ourselves," Karl says. "If you look out the window fifty years from now, we're going to be responsible for more of it."[11]

Some believers see serious consequences as a very real possibility. Dr. Wallace Broecker of Columbia University's Lamont-Doherty Earth Observatory writes that the climate system is "an angry beast, and we are poking it with sticks."[12] And a 1979 report signed by members of the influential National Academy of Sciences called global warming "the most serious environmental threat of the twenty-first century." The report warned that continued burning of fossil fuels "could have catastrophic consequences for climate, agriculture, plant and animal species, and coastlines worldwide."[13]

What the Dissenters Say

A small but vocal minority of climate experts is skeptical about the influence of human activities on global warming. Some of these dissenters say that global warming due to human activities is an unproven theory, not a fact, while others flat-out deny that there is any such thing as human-induced global warming.

Fred Singer is an atmospheric physicist who writes about environmental issues. Singer says there is no scientific consensus on whether human activities contribute to global warming. "Nor is there ever a scientific consensus, truly speaking, on any issue," he adds[14]. Singer is referring to the conservative nature of scientists in general, especially where new scientific claims are involved, and global warming is still a relatively new issue in the scientific community.

Another prominent dissenter about scientific consensus is Richard Lindzen, professor of meteorology at the Massachusetts Institute of Technology (MIT). Lindzen suggests that some scientists' attitudes toward the global-warming issue are shaped by decidedly unscientific factors.

Lindzen says that some scientists who claim they are believers are only responding to peer pressure from the majority of climate scientists.

Lindzen adds that politicians also exert pressure. "Some of the strongest proponents of global warming in Congress are also among the major supporters of science," he says[15]. These politicians exert an intimidating influence on scientists to agree that human-influenced global warming is a serious issue.

Dissenters dispute the widely accepted statistics that show global surface temperatures rising. They point to statistics gathered from weather balloons and satellites showing that the upper levels of the troposphere, the region of the atmosphere closest to Earth's surface, show little or no evidence of warming (see "Weather Satellites" on page 41). If global surface temperatures really were rising because of an increased greenhouse effect, then the troposphere would be warming as well, they claim.

Dissenters who dispute the global temperature increase also point to the *urban heat island (UHI) effect*. Some weather stations that monitor surface temperatures are located in and around large urban areas. With their acres of concrete and tall buildings, urban areas absorb more sunlight than the surrounding countryside, which means that their surface temperatures are bound to be consistently higher (see "Urban Heat Islands" on page 50). These urban readings artificially raise surface temperature statistics, dissenters claim.

Some dissenters do not dispute that global surface temperatures are increasing, but they do dispute that carbon dioxide emissions from human activities are the cause. Climate expert Jeffrey Salmon, who analyzes environmental issues for the George C. Marshall Institute in Washington, writes that there is "no solid scientific evidence to support the theory that Earth is warming because of man-made greenhouse gases."[16] Richard

Lindzen adds that in his opinion, rising surface temperature are not related to greenhouse gases. Lindzen also disputes the widely accepted notion among climate scientists that water vapor is a greenhouse gas. Not only does water vapor in the atmosphere not raise the temperature, Lindzen says, but it may actually lower it.

If the global temperature is increasing and greenhouse gases are not responsible, then what is the cause? Some dissenters, including Dr. William Gray, an atmospheric scientist at Colorado State University, say that the most likely cause is natural changes in the circulation of heat-bearing ocean waters. Other dissenters blame the warming on natural variations in the strength of solar radiation. If global temperature is rising, these dissenters say, the cause is natural, not man-made.

Predictions: Low to High

Predictions about how high global temperatures will rise by the year 2100 vary widely. The predictions that follow are based on the premise that carbon dioxide emissions will double by the end of the century. First, here are some dissenters' predictions of the average surface temperature increase during the twenty-first century.

- Robert Balling, climatologist at Arizona State University: less than 1° F (0.6° C)
- Fred Singer, atmospheric physicist: less than 1° F (0.6° C)
- Richard Lindzen, MIT professor: 0.5–2° F (0.3–1° C)
- Patrick Michaels, Professor of Meteorology at the University of Virginia: 2.3° F (1.3° C)[17]

Believers are less precise about their predictions. The Clinton administration's global warming report, issued in June 2000, predicted on the high side with an increase of 5–10° F (2.8–5.6° C) by 2100. Most climate scientists on the believer side predict a more modest increase of about 3.6° F (2° C) by 2100. Some believers predict that the increase in the Northern Hemisphere will be noticeably higher.

In later chapters, we will investigate what impacts these predicted temperature changes might have on the environment and on human society in the future. But first we'll look at the changes that human-induced global warming is making in the climate right now.

Signs of Climate Change

Taking Earth's Temperature

Tom Karl went to work for the National Climate Data Center (NCDC) in Asheville, North Carolina, in 1980, just as climate scientists were getting interested in global warming. Karl saw that while a great deal of recorded information on U.S. temperatures back to the mid-1800s existed in the NCDC archives, no one had tried to organize and analyze this information.

So between 1980 and 1986, Karl had all this U.S. weather data entered into a computer database. He also helped set up and launch a system for computerizing each new day's weather data. The primary source for this daily weather data is satellites.

Weather Satellites

Weather satellites scan the globe day and night, transmitting weather information such as temperatures, cloud formations, and wind patterns back to scientists. Nations that operate weather satellites include Japan, India, the former Soviet Union, and members of the European Space Agency, as well as the United States. These nations all share the information that they gather.

U.S. satellites are launched and managed by federal agencies. The National Aeronautics and Space Administration (NASA) builds and launches the satellites. The National Environmental Satellite Data and Information Service (NESDIS) distributes the information that satellites collect. NESDIS manages and distributes millions of bits of information each day. Some of it is

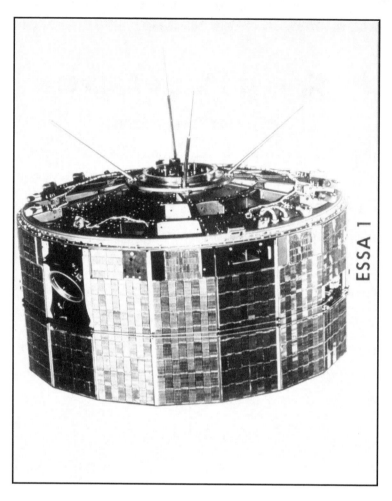

ESSA I, a TRIOS cartwheel satellite
launched on February 3, 1966.

beamed up to satellites from weather stations on Earth's surface, and some
is gathered directly by instruments onboard the satellites themselves.

Some of this information is in the form of images of Earth. Satellite
images have greatly improved since the first weather satellites were
launched in the 1960s. There are two types of satellite images: visible and
infrared. Visible images depend on sunshine reflecting back to the satellite
off clouds, landforms, and oceans. That's why visible images are taken only
during daylight hours. Infrared images, on the other hand, can be taken at

ny time because they depend upon infrared energy, which radiates by night as well as by day. Infrared imaging is especially useful for taking pictures of clouds at night.

Weather satellites also use microwave sounding unit (MSU) instruments to measure microwave radiation from clouds and air. This microwave information is used to track how air currents are moving and changing and how large-scale weather systems are developing.

GOES Satellites

GOES and POES are names for the two primary kinds of weather satellites. GOES stands for Geostationary Operational Environmental Satellites. NASA launched the first GOES in 1966. GOES circle Earth once every twenty-four hours along the equator at a speed exactly matching Earth's rotation. Therefore, they hover continuously over one position on Earth's surface. This is why they are called "geostationary."

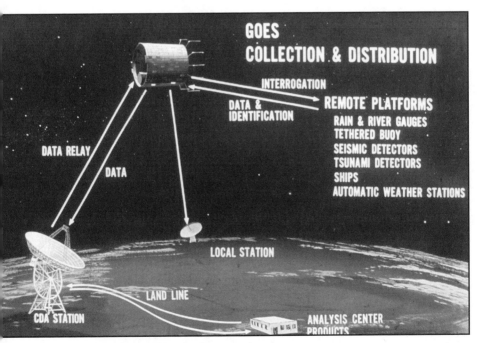

This graphic of GOES data shows the collection and distribution of an Applications Technology Satellite.

Two GOES are in orbit at a height of 22,300 miles (35,881 kilometers), and each one gives a picture of about a third of Earth's surface. One GOES monitors North and South America and most of the Atlantic Ocean; the other monitors North America and the Pacific Ocean basin.

Their primary data-gathering instruments are an imager and a sounder. The imager measures and maps sea-surface temperatures, wind speeds at the ocean surface, cloud-top temperatures, ground moisture, and land temperatures. Computers convert imager data into pictures. The sounder provides a vertical temperature and moisture profile of the atmosphere at various altitudes.

GOES are for "now-casting," or short-range weather forecasting. They detect severe weather conditions, such as tornadoes, flash floods, and hurricanes, and track their growth and movements from moment to moment.

Besides gathering environmental data, these satellites also act as clearing houses for data. Many weather stations all over Earth, known as surface platforms, beam their data up to GOES. These surface platforms include river and rain gauges, tide gauges, buoys, and automated weather stations on land and aboard ships at sea. GOES then beam this surface-platform data down to collecting stations on Earth, where it can be cataloged and analyzed.

POES Satellites

POES stands for Polar-Orbiting Operational Environmental Satellites. NASA launched the first POES in 1960. As with GOES, a new generation of POES is launched every decade or so, carrying the latest in advanced weather-recording instruments. There are two POES orbiting Earth. POES are positioned so that any data they report for any place on Earth are no more than six hours old.

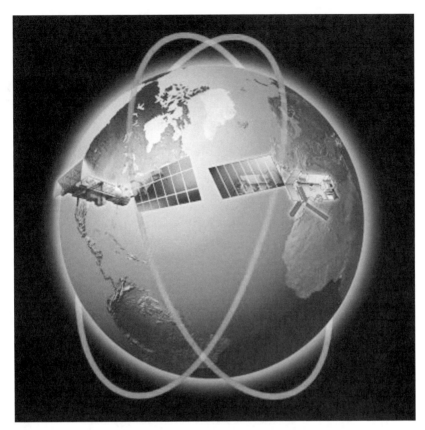

The complementary orbits of the U.S. NOAA and
European Metop POES.

While GOES travel in an east-to-west orbit around the equator,
POES travel in a north-to-south orbit over the North and South Poles.
They circle Earth every 90 minutes at a relatively low altitude of 300 to 800
miles (483 to 1,287 km). Instead of the whole-Earth images of GOES,
POES images show a 1,700-mile (2,735-km) width of ground and clouds.

While GOES are for short-term forecasting, POES are for long-term
forecasting. As they travel, POES scan the planet's surface with a radiome-
ter, which consists of a mirror, a telescope, and infrared- and visible-image
sensors that measure radiation levels. POES monitor sea and land surfaces
for temperature measurements. Like GOES, POES receive data as well as

gather it. This data is beamed up from surface platforms on land and at se
as well as from free-floating weather balloons and aircraft in flight.

Temperature Results

The data gathered and collected by weather satellites eventually reaches th
NCDC, where it is stored in a computer database. In 1998 the NCDC
began issuing monthly reports of global temperatures based on the analy
sis of this satellite data. These reports were ordered by Tom Karl, who wa
then the NCDC president.

Karl and his colleagues at the NCDC also began issuing reports tha
compared present and past global temperatures, using the information i
their carefully organized archives. Their first report revealed that in Januar
1998, the average global temperature was 0.5° F (0.3° C) warmer than i
was in January 1997. Since paleoclimatologists estimate that Earth's tem
perature has risen only 5 to 9° F (2.8 to 9.5° C) since the depths of the las
ice age 18,000–20,000 years ago, this was an alarming increase. (For mor
statistics about recent global temperature increases, (see "What the Fact
Say" on page 34.)

Other NCDC reports also show that the planet appears to be warm
ing significantly, but not in a regular, uniform manner. Temperature report
from the twentieth century show the following:

- Worldwide warming is uneven. The Northern Hemisphere is warmin
  at a faster rate than the Southern Hemisphere.
- Warming within the United States is also uneven. While worldwid
  warming since the 1800s was about 0.9° F (0.5° C), many regions of th
  United States have warmed much more than that, and a few hav
  actually cooled.
- Daily and seasonal warming also are uneven. Warming has been greate
  by night than by day and greater in winter than in summer.

Extreme Weather Events

Karl and other climate scientists who take Earth's temperature have found that, on the average, the temperature keeps rising. What effect do these rising temperatures have on Earth's weather? Some climate scientists believe that increasing temperatures mean more and more extreme weather events of all kinds, from floods to droughts and from tropical hurricanes to Arctic blizzards.

Karl and his colleagues at the NCDC have been gathering and analyzing information on extreme weather events since 1993. That was when they began looking back into NCDC archives and identifying instances of extreme heat, cold, drought, and storms. They defined "extreme" as the top and bottom 10 percent of the long-term climate record. For example, to make it onto the "extreme" list, a drought would have to last longer than 90 percent of all the dry stretches on record, and a rainstorm would have to dump more water than 90 percent of all the rainstorms on record.

They found that after 1970, precipitation averaged 5 percent more than in the previous seventy years. In some places the increase was as much as 20 percent, with the northeastern and midwestern parts of the country being the wettest. They also found that rainstorms and snowstorms were becoming heavier and more frequent.

Karl and his colleagues would not predict what this might mean for the climate in the future, but they did say that their findings indicated "a persistent increase of extreme events"[1] in the recent past and present.

El Niño and La Niña

Karl believes that global warming and the climate phenomena known as *El Niño* and *La Niña* may be connected. El Niño and La Niña are opposite and extreme phases of natural climate change that begin in the ocean. El

Niño is a 500-foot (152-m)-deep layer of warm water the size of Canada that appears now and then in the Pacific Ocean off the western coast of the Americas. The first people to recognize this phenomenon were Spanish-speaking fishermen along the coast of South America. They named it El Niño, "the Christ child," because it arrived around Christmas.

El Niño, which can last for years at a time, disrupts local climate patterns on land and sea. The impacts can be serious. The warm El Niño water that flows over cooler water causes more ocean water to evaporate into the atmosphere. This increased evaporation creates storms that dump vast amounts of water on Peru, causing devastating floods. And by covering the cooler water, which is much richer in nutrients, El Niño robs sea life of much-needed food and reduces the fish catch off the coast of South America.

El Niño also disrupts world climate patterns. It does this by altering the world's ocean and air currents, which distribute solar energy in the form of heat around the planet. Oceans are giant reservoirs of heat that influence global climate by heating and cooling the atmosphere above. This transfer of heat from ocean to air influences weather patterns across land and sea.

El Niño actually benefits people in some areas. The 1997–1998 El Niño, the largest on record at the time, saved people in the northern United States an estimated $5 billion in heating costs. It did this by influencing the polar jet stream, a river of the fastest moving air on the planet, into staying farther north than usual. El Niño contributed to making 1997 and 1998 two of the warmest years in U.S. climate history.

In May 1998, El Niño was replaced by its counterpart, La Niña, which is Spanish for "the girl child." While El Niño can raise the surface ocean temperature as much as 14° F (8° C) above normal, La Niña can lower it by nearly 8° F (4.5° C). La Niña brings colder, deep-sea water to the sur-

The NOAA has buoys that span the Pacific Ocean near the equator. They measure air, wind, and sea temperatures to collect La Niña and El Niño data.

face of the Pacific, making food for sea life plentiful and decreasing rainfall on Peru. This particular La Niña, the largest since the mid-twentieth century, persisted into the twenty-first century. During that time it was blamed for bringing droughts to the eastern and central United States and for causing hurricanes to slam into the Atlantic Coast.

While the increased presence of El Niño and La Niña cannot b directly attributed to global warming, some climate scientists believe ther may be a connection. Kevin Trenberth of the National Center fo Atmospheric Research says that global warming may be the cause of E Niño's more frequent appearances. Tom Karl of the NCDC says that E Niño and global warming together may be playing an important role i increasing the prevalence of extreme weather events.

To understand more about El Niños, the National Oceanic an Atmospheric Administration (NOAA) has launched a series of anchore buoys that span the Pacific Ocean near the equator, where El Niños sho up. These buoys measure the air and wind at the ocean surface as well a sea temperatures to a depth of 1,600 feet (488 m). These weather data ar transmitted by satellite to reporting stations, where they are made availabl to researchers and forecasters around the world.

If, as Karl and other climate scientists expect, El Niño and La Niña global warming, and extreme weather events are closely linked, the result gathered by the NOAA monitoring may help define this link.

Urban Heat Islands

The urban heat island (UHI) effect is another phenomenon that climate scientists are researching in relation to global warming. The term "urba heat island" refers to the differences in cooling and heating between th natural and human-made surfaces that make up a city.

Cities are hotter than rural areas because their surfaces are different. I cities, much of the soil and natural plant cover has been replaced b human-made surfaces. Tar, asphalt, brick, metal, glass, and concrete ar better conductors of heat than are soil and vegetation. In rural areas, th solar energy absorbed near the ground is put to work evaporating wate from the vegetation and soil. This evaporation helps to cool the surrounding air. In cities, on the other hand, buildings, streets, and sidewalks absorb the majority of solar energy that hits them and reradiate it in the form of infrared energy, further heating up the surrounding air. Asphalt roofs and parking lots, for example, soak up nearly all the radiation that hits them and reradiate it as heat. The canyons created by tall buildings facing one another on city streets add to the warmth by trapping and reflecting infrared energy back and forth between their walls. Waste heat and pollution generated by buildings, cars, buses, and trains make their way into the atmosphere, adding to the urban temperature increase. The UHI effect is especially noticeable after the Sun goes down, when heat that has been absorbed by human-made surfaces continues to be reradiated into the atmosphere.

This urban warming effect has been detected in cities with populations as small as 10,000, but it is more pronounced in larger cities. Phoenix, Arizona, is a case in point. In the summer, the city of Phoenix averages 9–11° F (5–6° C) warmer than the surrounding countryside. This difference can be as much as 11–14° F (6–8° C) in the early hours of calm, clear nights. Philadelphia, Pennsylvania, is another example. The temperature within the city averages 1.4° F (0.8° C) higher than the temperature at the airport, which is just 5 miles (8 km) outside the city limits.

Besides raising temperatures, the UHI effect increases precipitation levels. The UHI effect has become so pronounced in some urban areas that cities create their own weather. A study by NASA scientists in the late 1990s showed that Atlanta, Georgia, sometimes creates its own thunderstorms. The area hot air generated by this UHI can become so vast that it rises to form a dome above the city that is several degrees warmer than the surrounding countryside. When conditions are right, cooler air from the countryside rushes into the space left by this rising hot air, and the result i a thunderstorm.

Half the world's population already lives in cities, and this percentage will increase in years to come. Many climate scientists suspect tha the effects of UHIs will grow more extreme as cities keep growing and the planet's temperature keeps rising because of the enhanced greenhouse effect

Analyzing the Atmosphere

In addition to taking Earth's temperature, climate scientists are analyzing the changing composition of Earth's atmosphere. Their main interest is the atmospheric concentration of greenhouse gases, particularly carbon dioxide. How much is the atmospheric concentration of carbon dioxide increasing because of human activities?

Charles Keeling began measuring atmospheric carbon dioxide in 1957. Keeling's interest in CO_2 was not focused on global warming at first. As a student at the California Institute of Technology, Keeling set out to answer

Professor Charles D. Keeling in his laboratory at
the Scripps Institute of Oceanography in San Diego, California.

simple question: did the amount of carbon dioxide dissolved in lakes and rivers depend on the amount of carbon dioxide in the air?

Keeling's laboratory was in Pasadena, California. He took a hollow, glass sphere onto the roof of his lab and opened a valve. Air rushed into the vacuum he'd created in the sphere. Back in the lab, Keeling used liquid nitrogen to separate the carbon dioxide from the air he'd collected. Then he put the separated carbon dioxide into another instrument to get a reading.

His first reading from the roof of his Pasadena lab came to 310 parts of carbon dioxide per million (ppm). During the years to come, Keeling would take many more readings. The results would puzzle him at first. Later, they would astonish him. Keeling was to discover that some of the conventional thinking about how carbon dioxide and other gases in the atmosphere behaved was wrong. And his discoveries would play a dramatic role in the controversy over global warming that was yet to come.

Earth's Breathing

One of Keeling's discoveries concerned daily changes in carbon dioxide concentration. No one before him had ever set out to systematically measure the atmospheric concentration of carbon dioxide in a single spot during a twenty-four hour period. No one thought there would be any change.

But Keeling discovered that carbon dioxide concentration changes during the course of a day and that it changes on a regular basis. When the Sun rises, the concentration of carbon dioxide in the air decreases. Later in the day, as the Sun goes down, the concentration increases. Why does the carbon dioxide concentration change from night to day? The answer, Keeling realized, was photosynthesis. As the Sun rises, trees and other green plants begin absorbing carbon dioxide from the air. As the Sun sets, they stop performing photosynthesis and stop absorbing carbon dioxide. That's why carbon dioxide concentration cycles down and up regularly each day, as if the planet were breathing in during the day and breathing out at night.

Keeling discovered that carbon dioxide concentration also changes on a seasonal basis. The concentration decreases in the spring and summer when more trees and other green plants are growing and performing photosynthesis. The concentration increases in the fall and winter, when they release carbon dioxide as they die and decay.

Global Carbon Dioxide

Keeling also discovered that climate scientists were wrong in thinking that carbon dioxide concentration varied from place to place. He discovered this by taking readings in different places in the western United States, including Yellowstone National Park in Montana and the Big Sur area of northern California. He took readings in extremely remote places, including the 12,000-foot (3,658-m) Inyo Mountains in California, where gale-force winds were continually blowing, bringing in air from all sorts of different

The Inyo Mountains.

The Mauna Loa Weather Observatory in Hawaii measures
weather and atmospheric carbon dioxide.

places. If there were a spot on Earth where carbon dioxide readings would vary, it would be there.

But Keeling got the same readings 12,000 feet (3,658 m) above sea level that he got at sea level. No matter where he went, he always got the same reading: 315 ppm at mid-afternoon. Keeling had discovered that atmospheric circulation mixed the air so thoroughly that the concentration of carbon dioxide was the same everywhere, all around the world.

In March 1958, Keeling moved his research base to Mauna Loa Observatory in Hawaii, atop a volcanic mountain. There, far from human-made pollution, Keeling set up an experimental station for measuring carbon dioxide concentration on a systematic basis several times each day. After two years in Mauna Loa, Keeling had accumulated enough data to know that he had made another important discovery: the global concentration of carbon dioxide in the atmosphere was increasing. Each year the biosphere was inhaling and exhaling more and more carbon dioxide.

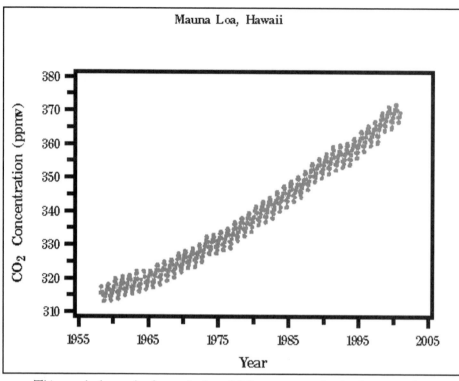

Mauna Loa, Hawaii

This graph shows the dramatic rise of CO_2 concentration in the atmosphere.

Keeling kept taking measurements at Mauna Loa. He found that, by the turn of the twenty-first century, atmospheric carbon dioxide concentration had risen from 315 ppm in the 1950s to 360 ppm, an increase of about 15 percent. How much carbon dioxide are human activities releasing into the atmosphere on a yearly basis? "At the end of World War II [1945], about a billion metric tons (1.1 tons) of carbon, in the form of CO_2, was being emitted to the atmosphere, "Keeling says. "When I started my measurements, it had risen to two and a half [billion metric tons (2.8 tons)]. At the present time [2000], it's almost seven [billion metric tons (7.7 tons)]."

Keeling has plotted the steady increase of carbon dioxide in the atmosphere. His early results drew a flood of skepticism, but even the most outspoken critics of global warming now accept his basic findings: oceans and forests cannot absorb the excess carbon dioxide that the burning of ossil fuels is releasing into the atmosphere, and the concentration of .tmospheric carbon dioxide is steadily increasing as a result.

Similar Results

Together, Tom Karl, Charles Keeling, and their colleagues have horoughly investigated Earth's surface temperature and the atmosphere's oncentration of carbon dioxide. Their findings show that as one has ncreased, so has the other. A majority of climate experts see these two imultaneous increases as more than a coincidence. These scientists see the urrent increase in global carbon dioxide concentrations as a direct cause of he current increase in global temperatures. Few climate experts dispute his conclusion.

But some dissenters claim that this current global temperature increase has decidedly positive impacts on both the environment and human soci- ty. They point out that more CO_2 means more photosynthesis, which neans more plant growth. Fred Singer says, "What is the impact on agri- ulture? The answer is, it's positive. It's good. What's the impact on forests of greater levels of CO_2 and greater temperatures? It's good. What is the mpact on water supplies? It's neutral. What is the impact on recreation? It's mixed. You get, on the one hand, perhaps less skiing. On the other hand, you get more sunshine and maybe better beach weather."[3]

The dissenters say that the global temperature increase is at worst a minor annoyance and at best a real positive. One of the positives they point to is the impact of higher concentrations of atmospheric carbon dioxide on plant life.

Impacts on Plant Life

Fred Palmer, a spokesman for Western Fuels Association, a non profit cooperative that supplies coal to power plants, says that enhanced levels of carbon dioxide from the burning of fossil fuels is fertilizing the soil, no polluting it. Climate scientists are performing a large-scale experiment to test this theory. They have set up rings of carbon dioxide pumping station around sections of fourteen-year-old pine forest near Durham, North Carolina. Towers ringing each section of trees pump compressed carbon dioxide from tanker trucks into the air from all sides twenty-four hours day, 365 days a year.

This pumping raises the level of atmospheric carbon dioxide concentration in each section of trees to 560 ppm, the rate it is predicted to reach by the year 2050. As a result, say the scientists, the rate of photosynthesis in this "forest of the future" has been increased by 50 to 60 percent. During the first two years of the experiment, from 1996 to 1998, the trees exposed to the enhanced carbon dioxide grew at a 25 percent faster rate than the surrounding trees. These results strongly suggest that global warming caused by an enhanced greenhouse effect really does increase plant growth as Palmer and Singer claim.

Impacts on Wildlife

Keeling's analysis of carbon dioxide readings shows that as the percentage of carbon dioxide has increased and global temperature has risen, the seasons have changed. Spring warmth is arriving earlier in the Northern Hemisphere, and summer heat is lasting longer. The total difference is about twelve days, with the time evenly split: about six more days of spring and six more of summer. As Singer says, this change is good for agriculture. Farmers in many parts of the Northern Hemisphere now have a longer growing season for their crops.

But what is the effect on wildlife? Since animals take their cues for how to behave from the climate, some species are being forced to change their

An Edith's checkerspot butterfly.

habits. Birds are altering their migration patterns. American robins are coming back from their southern wintering grounds to their northern breeding grounds earlier in the year. Some birds are even staying north for the entire winter now that the climate is more moderate.

Some species of butterflies are adapting to the global temperature increase by shifting their ranges northward. One study in particular

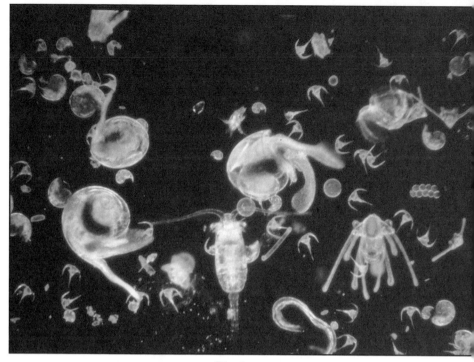

Plankton.

carefully documents how one butterfly species, known as Edith's checkerspot, is adapting. Biologist Camille Parmesan spent fourteen months driving 45,000 miles (72,405 km) through western North America from
Mexico to Canada, covering the species' entire range. Her study showed
that the Edith's checkerspot butterfly was moving steadily northward with
the climate, deserting its southern extremes in Mexico and inhabiting new
places farther north in Canada. Parmesan also found that the Edith's
checkerspot butterflies that lived on mountains were moving to higher elevations, where temperatures were cooler.

Another larger study in Europe showed similar results. Butterflies of
thirty-five different species were permanently relocating to higher latitudes
and higher elevations in order to establish new ranges that matched their
old ranges in temperature. As the climate shifts northward and upward, the
butterflies appear to be shifting with it. Parmesan won't say for sure that

Marmots.

this shift is caused by global warming, but "what I can say is that it is exactly what is predicted from global warming scenarios."[4]

Some species of wildlife are less successful at adapting to new climates than birds and butterflies. Climate changes are throwing some animals' worlds out of whack. A case in point is marine life off the coast of southern California. Researchers link the disappearance of the marine life known as *plankton* to a 2–3° F (1–1.7° C) increase in surface water temperature since the 1950s. The nutrients that plankton need to survive do not exist in such warm waters. The disappearance of plankton has led to a decline in fish, which feed off the plankton, and in seabirds and seals, which feed off the fish. A slight warming of ocean waters has upset all these animals' lives.

Another case in point is the marmot, a thick-bodied rodent that resembles a squirrel. Marmots live at high altitudes and hibernate for up to eight months of the year. Their response to the warming of the climate has been to emerge from hibernation up to a month earlier than they had in previous years. Marmots used to find the snow melted and the vegetation they depend on for food already growing when they emerged from their long winter's nap. But now, because they emerge so much earlier, the snow pack is still intact. Temperatures are higher, but not high enough to melt the snow. Meanwhile, the marmots have nothing to eat, and studies have shown that some of them starve before the snow melts and plants appear.

Like all wildlife species, marmots depend on the *ecosystem* for survival. If they change their habits due to climate change before other parts of the ecosystem change, they may find themselves in a world that doesn't work for them anymore.

Polar Extremes

To examine the extremes of climate-change impact, scientists look to the poles. Studies have shown that climate changes are more extreme in these polar regions than anywhere else on Earth. In the Arctic, summers have gotten longer and warmer. In Fairbanks, Alaska, summer days are now 11 percent warmer than they were in the 1960s. Minimum temperatures are rising, snow cover is decreasing, permafrost is thawing, and glaciers are melting. Researchers have found that soil and surface temperatures in the Arctic increased by 4 to 9° F (2 to 5° C) during the twentieth century.

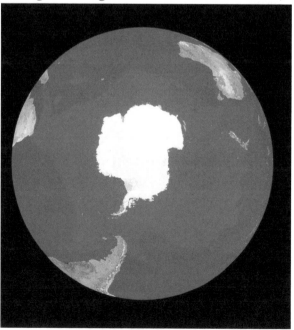

A satellite image of Antarctica
and the southern ocean.

This temperature increase in the Arctic affects plants and soil. As more ice melts because of rising temperatures, plants that had been frozen in the ice long ago, before they could decay, are now exposed to the air and sunlight. As they decay, these newly exposed plants release more carbon dioxide into the atmosphere, which adds to the greenhouse effect, which makes even more ice melt. As more ice melts, more of the dark soil that had been covered by ice is also exposed. Soil tends to absorb sunlight, while ice tends to reflect it back into space. As the newly exposed soil absorbs more sunlight, the surface temperature rises, which results in more ice melting, which exposes more soil and plants, and so on.

Similar changes are taking place in the Antarctic, which may be the place on the planet most affected by global warming. Its warming rates are up to ten times the global average. This warming is affecting polar wildlife. Like the birds and butterflies of Europe and the Americas, polar animals are changing their ranges. While this means a northward movement in the Northern Hemisphere, in the Southern Hemisphere it means that animals are moving farther south. Seals and penguins are showing up in regions farther south in the Antarctic than ever before. Scientists stationed there say the warming climate in these traditionally colder areas is the only explanation for this sudden southward migration.

While warmer temperatures are generally welcome in areas such as northern Europe and the American Midwest, they raise alarms in polar regions. The reason is the thousands of square miles of ice. Scientists are taking satellite readings, setting up observation posts, and spending months at a time in remote stretches of the Antarctic ice cap to assess the impact of global warming on it. They have found that the Antarctic ice cap is starting to break up in several places. Five of the nine ice shelves attached to the Antarctic Peninsula have disintegrated. Cameras aboard an orbiting

POES satellite spotted a broken-off piece of the Ross ice shelf the size of Jamaica. In 1995 scientists found that the Larsen ice shelf had started disintegrating. By 2000 nearly 1,000 square miles (2,590 sq km) of the Larsen ice shelf had collapsed into the ocean, while thousands of square miles more appeared ready to go.

Scientists are seeing similar impacts in Arctic regions. From data collected by nuclear submarines in the Arctic Ocean, scientists estimate that the Arctic ice cap has thinned by 40 percent since the 1970s.

Sea Levels

This thinning and melting of ice in polar regions raises alarms because it signals a further rise in global sea levels. According to an IPCC report issued in April 2001, global sea levels rose an average of 4 to 8 inches (10 to 20 centimeters) during the twentieth century. Scientists have identified two primary causes for this rise: thermal expansion of the upper layers of ocean water and the melting of polar ice and mountain glaciers, both caused by global warming. One climate scientist puts it this way: "Sea-level rise is the dipstick of climate change." Global warming and rising seas are "pretty much hardwired" together[5].

In the United States, the most extreme sea-level rise has come in the Mississippi Delta region of Louisiana, which has experienced a rise of an entire meter (3.3 feet) in the past century. Louisiana contains 40 percent of the coastal wetlands in the continental United States. Rising sea levels are submerging Louisiana's coastal marshes, where the addition of organic matter and mineral sediment from the Mississippi River can no longer keep pace with sea-level rise. Scientists call this situation "sediment budget deficit." As long as this deficit situation continues, marshes will continue to vanish, and so will the fish and wildlife that live there.

Louisiana coastal marshes.

Besides damaging wildlife, flooding damages property. In the United States, 53 percent of the population lives in coastal counties, and that percentage is rising. Each week an average of 8,700 new single-family homes are constructed along U.S. coasts. So far, damage to property due to rising sea levels has been small. Like other industrialized nations, the United States has wealth and technology it can use to minimize damage due to sea-level rise.

But some poorer nations with fewer technological resources at their command see more global sea-level rise as a serious threat to their existence. This is especially true of low-lying island nations such as Tuvalu and the Republic of Maldives. Tuvalu is a tiny country of ten thousand people that is composed of nine low-lying coral atolls in the South Pacific. A Tuvalu government official warns, "The question of total migration—evacuation—is looming."[6] The Republic of Maldives is composed of 1,200 tiny, low-lying islands in the Indian Ocean. A government official from that nation warns, "The impact of global warming and climate change can effectively kill us off, make us refugees, lose every bit of land that we have available to us right now."[7]

But will sea levels continue to rise this century? And if so, by how much? Will they rise enough to threaten low-lying island nations and the coastal areas of larger nations? Climate scientists are looking for answers to these and other crucial questions about Earth's future during the twenty-first century.

Chapter 5

Forecasting the Extent of Climate Change

To forecast future climates, scientists use *general circulation models (GCMs)*. GCMs are computer software programs that run on super-powerful computers. They are something like computer *simulation* games. In one popular simulation game, the player is responsible for building and running a model city. The player builds roads and houses and plans everything from garbage collection to traffic management to education. The player's goal is to create a model city that operates the way a real-world city operates.

Creating a General Circulation Model

Instead of simulating cities, GCMs simulate the circulation patterns of the atmosphere and oceans. The purpose of GCMs is to show how major changes in the atmosphere, such as an increase in atmospheric carbon dioxide, might affect the climate. GCMs examine long-term climate trends and the climate's responses to major changes.

To create a GCM, scientists first build a working model of the actual climate. This climate model is made of components known as mini-models, such as:

- a mini-model of Earth's oceans that includes the temperatures of the water at different depths and the movements of the currents that circulate hot and cold ocean water around the world

- a mini-model of Earth's atmosphere that includes the concentrations of the various greenhouse gases, the temperature of the air at different altitudes, the formation of clouds, and the movements of the currents that carry hot and cold air around the world

- a mini-model of Earth's landmasses that includes each of the different surface types, such as cities, forests, farmland, and deserts, and the amount of evaporation that occurs in each surface type

- a mini-model of the ice caps at the North and South Poles that includes the different thicknesses of ice and snow and their capacity to absorb incoming sunlight and reflect it back into the air

Once these individual mini-models are created, scientists put them all together into a GCM software program. The program contains all the "knowns," that is, all the factors that account for Earth's natural climate.

Testing a Global Circulation Model

The assembled model must pass certain tests before it can be certified as ready for use. In one test the model is run against the current climate. Will it accurately reflect the climate as it is right now? Another test is called "hindcasting," or backward forecasting. This means running the model against what scientists know about past climates. Can it accurately "predict" climate changes that scientists know actually happened in the past?

Sometimes this testing goes on for years. That's because GCMs are complex creations. A typical GCM will contain dozens of different mini-models, each containing thousands of computer instructions. And each one of these mini-models and the thousands of instructions that make it up must be fine-tuned. Scientists must adjust these instructions and test them again and again until the model is as accurate and reliable as they can make it. Only then is it ready for use.

Running a General Circulation Model

The purpose of a GCM is to attempt to predict the impact that human activities will have on Earth's future climate. Scientists can't know exactly what these future human-made impacts will be. For example, they can't know how many tons of carbon dioxide the world's population will be releasing into the atmosphere in the year 2100 or what impacts they will have on Earth's climate. So scientists must make the best educated guesses they can, based on the most accurate information they can collect.

Once scientists have made their best guesses, they turn them into *scenarios*, which are possible future outcomes. Two common scenarios, for example, predict that, by the year 2100, Earth's population will have increased from the present 6 billion people to around 12 billion, and because of the continued burning of fossil fuels, the concentration of atmospheric carbon dioxide will have risen from its present 360 ppm to 720 ppm.

Scientists then program these new scenarios into their GCM software. Let's say they program in the two scenarios above. The climate that the model predicts for 2100 will now look different from the climate it would have predicted without those scenarios.

How different? To find out, scientists run the new GCM program and wait for the results. Because the programs are so complex, scientists must wait days or even weeks for the super-computers to produce their results. These results will suggest answers to questions such as the following:

- With twice as much carbon dioxide in the atmosphere, how much will global temperatures increase?
- What will this temperature increase do to the polar ice caps?
- Will this temperature increase raise sea levels around the world?
- What will this temperature increase do to the amount of worldwide precipitation?

- What will this increase do to the frequency of extreme weather events such as hurricanes and blizzards?
- What impacts will this increase have on plants and wildlife on the land and in the seas?
- What impacts will this increase have on human societies?

Conflicting Results

At present there are about twenty GCM super-computer modeling stations in the world, located in England, Germany, Japan, and the United States. If you were to program the same scenarios into each of them and set them all running, each model would give you a different set of results.

These conflicting results are not the fault of the scientists who create GCMs. The problem lies in the nature of the climate. Earth's climate is far too complex and unpredictable for any computer to accurately represent. No computer on Earth is powerful enough to perform all the calculations it would take to accurately represent all the interacting components of Earth's climate, and scientists doubt that such a computer will ever exist.

But even if a computer powerful enough to accurately represent Earth's climate did exist, the information it would require to do the job is not available. Scientists don't know enough about Earth's climate to tell a computer how to accurately represent it. For example, GCMs are weak on representing how the atmosphere and the ocean exchange heat, because scientists know relatively little about how this heat exchange works. This means that the scientists creating these models must make the best educated guesses they can about factors such as atmosphere–ocean heat exchange. And until scientists know a great deal more about how the climate works, they will have to keep relying on educated guesses that result in GCMs that give different results.

The Chaos Factor

GCMs can't give perfect predictions for another reason: the element of unpredictability built into the climate. Let's say that scientists have somehow learned all there is to learn about the climate. And let's say that they have used that knowledge to create a GCM program that perfectly represents all the complex, day-to-day workings of Earth's climate. And let's say they have access to a super-computer powerful enough to run a program that includes all this knowledge. Would they then possess the knowledge and power to predict the climate's future?

They would not, because natural events that no scientists could have predicted would unexpectedly pop up and throw off their predictions. Scientists have a name for these unexpected natural events. They refer to them as the *chaos factor* because they occur chaotically, with no warning and with no apparent pattern. The climate system is so sensitive that any natural disturbance can affect it for years on end.

El Niño and La Niña are examples of the chaos factor at work (see "El Niño and La Niña" on page 47). Climate scientists cannot predict when these natural phenomena will appear, how long they will last, or how strong and long-lasting an effect they will have on global climate. Because these events can't be predicted ahead of time, they can't be programmed into a GCM. And because they can't be programmed into a model, they are bound to disrupt the model's predictions.

Other examples of the chaos effect are hurricanes, earthquakes, and volcanic eruptions. The eruption of Mount Pinatubo in the Philippines in 1991 is a dramatic example of the chaos factor at work. Let's say you were a climate scientist in 1981, trying to predict what the climate would be like ten years in the future. You could not possibly have known that in 1991 this inactive volcano would suddenly launch 30 trillion pounds (13.5 trillion kilograms) of rock, dust, liquid, and gas into the air. You could not have known that the result would be 40 billion pounds (18 billion km) of sulfur dioxide gas rising into the atmosphere or that, two years later, 30 percent of this volcanic gas would remain in the air.

The result of this chaotic natural event was a sudden global cooling. Volcanic gas cools the atmosphere by bouncing sunlight back into space: the greenhouse effect in reverse. Because of the gases from the eruption, global temperature actually cooled by 1° F (0.6° C) for the next three years. Then, in 1994, after the effects of the eruption had died out, Earth's temperature began rising again and continued rising all through the 1990s and into the twenty-first century.

Patterns in GCM Results

No GCM can account for the chaos factor. This and other shortcomings— shortages of computer power and of knowledge about the climate—mean

Richard Lindzen.

that GCMs are imperfect tools for predicting future climates. Does this mean that scientists who make their GCM results public are behaving irresponsibly?

Some climate scientists, such as Richard Lindzen, think so. Lindzen is concerned about the public reaction to frightening GCM predictions, such as the possibility of sea levels rising dramatically during the twenty-first century. Even though models are unreliable, Lindzen says, the public tends to "hold in awe anything that emerges from a sufficiently large computer." Referring to individual GCM results, he asks, "Should scientists publicize such predictions since the models are almost certainly wrong?"[1]

Climate scientists who work with GCMs are quick to admit their models' shortcomings. They agree that even the most powerful computers on Earth are not yet sufficiently powerful and that too little is known about global climate to get accurate predictions from any single model.

But that doesn't mean that GCMs are necessarily wrong, as Lindzen implies—not when their differing results are looked at as a whole. Most climate scientists don't judge these models one at a time. Instead, they look at the results of all the models. As they analyze these results, they remain on the lookout for similarities and for overall patterns.

In the 1990s Tom Karl and his colleagues at the NCDC analyzed past GCM predictions. Their analysis showed that GCMs were inconsistent in terms of predicting specific changes in temperatures and precipitation levels. But their analysis also showed that models consistently predicted the same overall trends. GCMs agreed that a warming climate in northern latitudes would result in

- more intense droughts
- more intense rainstorms
- warmer nights and winters
- summers more like they are in the tropics, with little difference between temperatures from one day to the next

How accurate were these predictions of overall trends? When Karl and his colleagues compared past GCM predictions with U.S. temperature records from 1976 through 1994, they found that the models were remarkably on target. The warming climate during those years actually had produced more intense droughts and rainstorms as well as warmer nights and winters in the northern latitudes. And day-to-day temperatures in summer in the northern latitudes really had become more even, just as the GCM had predicted.

Climate scientists who work with GCMs admit that their prediction cannot be relied upon to be exact. But they do believe that these model can be relied upon to give broad indications of where Earth's climate is headed. Those broad indications point to a continued global warming leading to significant impacts on both the environment and human society. Climate scientist John Houghton writes, "Although we are not yet very confident regarding detailed [GCM] predictions, enough is known to realize that the rate of climate change due to increasing greenhouse gases will almost certainly bring substantial deleterious [harmful] effects and pose a large problem to the world."[2]

Chapter 6

Forecasting the Impacts of Climate Change

Most climate experts believe that human-induced global warming will continue at least through the end of the twenty-first century. Even if we were to cut down drastically on the burning of fossil fuels, scientists say, the extra carbon dioxide already present in the atmosphere will remain there and continue to increase global temperatures until at least 2100. If we accept this majority outlook, then we need to examine how global warming might impact our lives and how to deal with those potential impacts.

So far we have looked at the first three steps in dealing with global warming.

Step 1: Gather data about Earth's past and present climate.

Step 2: Gather data on how human activities are changing the climate.

Step 3: Use this data in climate models to forecast likely alternatives for how the climate could change.

Now we will look at step 4: examine the impacts that those climate changes might bring.

The first three steps involve climate scientists. This fourth step brings new kinds of experts into the process, such as economists, biologists, plant geneticists, chemists, physicists, engineers, hydrologists, agronomists, and architects. All of these different experts are needed to design and use the tools for assessing the likely impacts of global warming.

The tools they will use are known as *integrated assessment models (IAMs)*. Like GCMs, IAMs are computer software programs designed to simulate the future in terms of climate change. Like GCMs, IAMs are meant not to predict the future but to give a range of likely alternatives. They do this by picking up where GCMs leave off. For example, if a GCM predicts that sea levels could rise by as much as 3 feet (1 m) during this century, an IAM might begin with that scenario and ask: what are the likely impacts of a 3-foot (1-m) sea-level rise? What sort of ecological damage could it do? How much property damage might result? How many people might lose their homes? Their jobs? Their lives?

To find answers to questions like these, the people who create IAMs follow the same basic steps as GCM creators. They gather data, program them into computer software, and run the software on super-computers. Then they analyze the results and draw their conclusions.

The U.S. National Assessment

We can get an idea of how IAMs work by looking at the United States Global Climate Report Project (USGCRP). This ongoing IAM project was mandated by an act of Congress called the Global Change Research Act of 1990. Its stated purpose reminds us of how truly global the impacts of global warming can be. USGCRP's purpose is to "analyze the effects of global change on the natural environment, agriculture, energy production and use, land and water resources, transportation, human health and welfare, human social systems, and biological diversity" as well as "current

rends in global change, both human-induced and natural," for the twen-
y-first century.[1]

This ongoing IAM project assesses the impact of climate change from
hree perspectives: regional analysis, sectoral analysis, and a national syn-
hesis. Regional IAMs analyze geographic regions of the United States,
wenty in all, such as the mid-Atlantic and the Southeast. Sectoral IAMs
analyze important goods and services, such as agriculture, water, forests,
coastal areas, and marine resources, as well as human health. The third perspective, national synthesis, means putting together regional and sectoral
analyses to create "a national assessment on the potential consequences of
climate variability and change for the nation."[2]

USGCRP analyses are intended for *policy makers*. A policy maker is
anyone in a position of authority whose job it is to make vital decisions on
matters that affect great numbers of people. This includes government officials at the federal, state, and local levels, as well as heads of insurance and
pharmaceutical companies, law and engineering firms, farm cooperatives,
fisheries, energy corporations, and hospitals.

The U.S. Congress is the primary audience for USGCRP's national
synthesis because Congress is ultimately responsible for passing laws
addressing the consequences of global warming on a national level.
Regional analyses are intended for state, county, and city governments,
while a particular sectoral analysis will be of interest to policy makers
involved in that particular sector of the economy.

Regional Analyses

A regional analysis looks at how global warming might affect a given
region of the nation. A USGCRP regional analysis of the Southeast, which
includes the eastern and Gulf coasts, shows this region to be the most
vulnerable of all to the effects of global warming. The region from the

Virginia–South Carolina border to the Texas-Mexico border contains 8 percent of U.S. coastal wetlands and 50 percent of U.S. barrier islands. Th puts the region at extremely high risk from possible rises in sea level due t global warming.

A USGCRP analysis of the mid-Atlantic region, which includes all c parts of eight states from New York to North Carolina, gives somewhat les ominous results. It shows that the region is likely to continue to becom warmer and wetter in this century and that coastal areas are likely to remai at high risk of damage from sea-level rise.

Sectoral Analyses

A sectoral analysis looks at the impacts of global warming on a given sec tor of the economy. For example, a sectoral analysis focusing on forest helps state officials make plans for keeping their state's economy healthy. I also helps lumber company executives make plans for keeping their busi nesses profitable in the years to come.

For example, GCM results show that the growth rate of forests in th Northern Hemisphere during this century is expected to increase by abou 20 percent due to increased atmospheric carbon dioxide concentration (se "Impacts on Plant Life" on page 57). IAM results show that this could b both good news and bad news for states such as Washington and Oregor which depend heavily on the lumber industry for jobs. If more timber i going to be available, then more people will be needed to cut it down an turn it into lumber, and that means more jobs. But IAM results also shov that this 20 percent increase in available timber means that timber price will decrease, which could lead to a serious loss in revenue, which coul lead to a serious loss of jobs.

Sectoral analyses that focus on agriculture look at the impacts of cli mate change on crop production to give farmers the information they wil need to manage their crops in the face of climate change. These agricultural IAMs play different roles in different nations. Let's say that GCMs predict a warmer, drier climate. In a richer, industrialized nation such as the United States, this kind of climate change could mean that farms will fail and farmers will lose income. But in a poorer, developing nation such as Mali in western Africa, where the majority of people are *subsistence farmers* who grow their own food and just enough of it to survive, this climate change could lead to mass starvation.

Besides warning farmers of potential problems, agricultural IAMs can help them solve those problems. An agricultural IAM can simulate how well different varieties of crops grow in different climates. The results can help biologists develop new crops that farmers could grow in warmer, drier climates.

USGCRP reports on IAM studies will be released on a continuing basis in years to come. While these sectoral and regional analyses do not suggest ready-made solutions, they do identify potential problems and sometimes point the way toward potential solutions.

Drawbacks of Integrated Assessment Models

IAM analyses are indications, not predictions. Like GCMs, IAMs can only point the way, not pinpoint it. IAMs are notably weak when it comes to predicting the following:

- the rate at which human activities are changing the climate
- the kinds of climate changes that human activities cause
- reactions of different parts of the ecosystem to climate changes
- how climate changes impact human society
- how the chaos factor throws off predictions

Like the creators of GCMs, creators of IAMs must operate with imperfect information. Sometimes they must rely on educated guesses instead of scientific facts. This leads to the same sort of controversy as with GCMs. These assessments are unreliable, say critics. They shouldn't be used until they operate solely on the basis of fact.

True, says the pro-IAM side; these models are not entirely reliable. But IAMs are created to speculate on the future, not predict it. IAM supporters say that these assessments are the best tools we have for assessing the possible impacts of future global warming and evaluating possible responses to those impacts.

This book began by mentioning a few of the possible impacts of global warming on human society, both good news and bad news, as predicted by climate experts (see the introduction on page 7). Now that we have examined the tools that climate experts use to predict future global warming and its impacts, let's take a closer look at those possible predicted impacts on a worldwide basis.

Possible Impacts on the Land

As mentioned in "Impacts on Plant Life" on page 57, carbon dioxide is needed for photosynthesis. The more carbon dioxide there is in the air, the faster plants will grow. Experiments have confirmed that forests will grow at a faster rate because of increased carbon dioxide in the atmosphere from fossil-fuel emissions. That's a positive effect of global warming. But, according to IAM studies, some forests may actually die out as a result of other factors associated with global warming. One reason forests may die is that warmer climates also mean more insects. For example, forests in Alaska are now dying due to an explosion of the insect population. A third to half of Alaska's white spruce trees have died from attacks of the bark beetle, which thrives in the warmer climate.

Another potential downside to global warming for the world's forests is climate shift. According to studies produced by the IPCC, climate zones

An Alaskan white spruce.

in the Northern Hemisphere are expected to shift northward during the twenty-first century by 100 to 350 miles (161 to 563 km) and upward in altitude by 500 to 1,800 feet (152 to 549 m) (see "Impacts on Wildlife" on page 58). This climate shift is taking place too quickly for trees to migrate northward and upward with the climate in which they thrive. As a result, according to one study, up to one-third of the world's forests may die out during this century.

Weeds already blanket areas previously inhabited by trees and grass-lands that have been destroyed by a too-warm climate. Other areas are turning into deserts, notably in poorer, developing nations such as Mali in western Africa, where cropland is already desperately scarce.

More floods are also predicted in some developing nations, such as Bangladesh and Indonesia. Extreme weather events, including cyclones, hurricanes, floods, and droughts, are predicted to increase in general and to cause more damage in developing nations than in industrialized ones such as the United States.

Possible Impacts on the Oceans: The Conveyor Belt

Some climate studies suggest that increased global warming during this century may actually lead to extreme global cooling. The Northern Hemisphere could actually cool drastically if what scientists call the ocean's *conveyor-belt mechanism* were to shut down due to global warming. This so-called conveyor-belt mechanism is what carries warm ocean water from the tropics toward the poles and back again.

The atmosphere and the oceans circulate heat around the world. The atmosphere moves heat along in rivers of air. In a similar manner, powerful ocean currents carry warm water northward and southward from the tropics, warming the air and land as they flow toward the Poles. In the Northern Hemisphere, the Atlantic Ocean carries warm water northward thousands of miles from the tropics, delivering 30 percent as much heat as the Sun and keeping northern Europe several degrees warmer than it would be otherwise.

As this warm ocean water flows northward, it cools, which makes it denser. When it reaches the North Atlantic, approaching Greenland, this upper-level water starts to sink because it is so cool. It also sinks for another reason: the upper layers of the oceans are saltier than the lower layers, and salt water is denser than fresh water. From here, near Greenland, these salty layers of cool ocean water travel southward in a return flow, like a conveyor belt.

Paleoclimatologists have found evidence suggesting that this conveyor-belt mechanism has broken down several times in the distant past. The cause was a vast surplus of fresh, unsalty water dumped into the North Atlantic. This fresh water came from ice sheets melted by the warmer temperatures and from increased evaporation that led to increased precipitation, also caused by warmer temperatures.

This vast surplus of freshwater diluted the waters of the North Atlantic at the northern end of this conveyor-belt mechanism, making them much less salty. With less salt, these surface waters became less dense and lighter, until they became so light that they stopped sinking and stopped recirculating southward. When this happened, the great ocean conveyor-belt mechanism shut down.

With no more rivers of warm water flowing northward from the tropics, the 30 percent supply of extra heat to northern Europe shut down, too. As a result, the climate turned so cold that Ireland took on the climate of the Arctic Circle and much of northern Europe became uninhabitable. The chances of this actually happening during this century are seen as remote, but not impossible.

Possible Impacts on the Oceans: Sea-Level Rise

As global temperatures increase, ocean waters warm up and expand in volume, which means that the same amount of water will take up more space. In addition, melting polar ice will put more freshwater into the oceans. The result is rising sea levels. During the last century, sea levels rose 4 to 10 inches (10 to 25 centimeters). During this century they are predicted to rise anywhere between 0 and 4 feet (1.3 m).

Scientists say that a 1-foot (30.5-cm) rise in sea level would push shorelines inland as far as 1,000 feet (305 m). This could threaten entire cities. David Gardiner of the Environmental Protection Agency says that sea-level rise during this century "could drown up to 60 percent of ou[r] coastal wetlands" and "inundate more than 5,000 square miles (12,950 s[q] km), an area the size of Connecticut, of dry land in the United States if n[o] protective actions are taken."[3]

Some climate scientists foresee even more drastic outcomes. If globa[l] warming were to cause the Antarctic ice sheet and the Greenland ice ca[p] to collapse, sea levels worldwide could rise by as much as 20 feet (6 m). Th[e] chances of such a catastrophe actually happening are remote, bu[t] the possible consequences could mean that hundreds of millions of peopl[e] worldwide would be hit by flooding. Florida's coastal cities would b[e] underwater, as would the Florida Keys and all of southern Florida. Muc[h] of New York City would be submerged, and island nations such as th[e] Bahamas, Tuvalu, and the Republic of Maldives would cease to exist.

Possible Impacts on Human Health

A report by the IPCC states, "Climate change is likely to have wide-rang[-]ing and mostly adverse impacts on human health, with significant loss o[f] life."[4] One of these impacts is the spread of infectious diseases carried b[y] insects, such as malaria, dengue, and yellow fever. According to the Unite[d] Nations Environment Program (UNEP), even a slight rise in global tem[-]perature could trigger explosions of Earth's insect populations.

Among the insects likely to multiply is the mosquito species *Aede[s] aegypti*, which spreads dengue fever and yellow fever. Populations of *Aede[s] aegypti* have already begun appearing at higher elevations than ever befor[e] in Central and South America. Like butterflies and birds, these mosquitoe[s] are migrating to new habitats as the warming climate shifts. Malaria-bearing mosquitoes of central Africa and Asia have also been changing

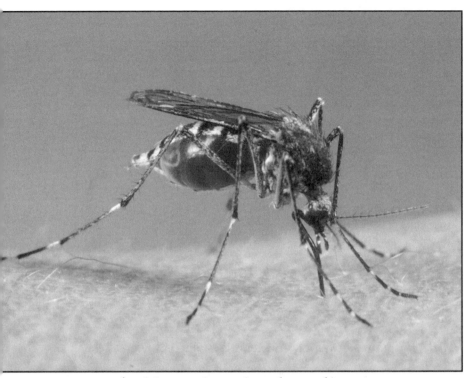

An *Aedes aegypti* mosquito on human skin.

their habitat ranges. Some of the areas in which these mosquitoes are appearing have been free of malaria for decades. "There is a real risk of reintroducing malaria into nonmalarial areas, including Australia, the U.S., and southern Europe," say IPCC researchers[5].

Diseases carried by water, such as cholera and hepatitis, are also predicted. These potentially fatal diseases, which are carried by sewage and floodwaters, are likely to spread if precipitation brought on by warmer temperatures becomes as frequent and severe as some climate scientists predict.

Social Dislocation

We have looked at what might happen to wildlife and plants that can't adapt quickly enough to global warming. What about human beings? John

Houghton of the IPCC writes that, during the twenty-first century, "Th rate of climate change is likely to be large, probably greater than Earth ha seen for many millennia. Many ecosystems (including human beings) ma not be able to adapt easily to such a rate of change."[6]

For people in poorer, developing countries, such as the nation of sub-Saharan Africa, the consequences could be devastating. The popu lations of some of these nations are already poised on the brink o starvation. If global warming were to hit them with a combination o severe-weather damage, drought, flood, and infectious disease, tens or eve hundreds of millions of environmental refugees could be created in a ver short time. These landless, homeless people would then have to resort to roaming Earth in search of food and shelter. No industrialized nation o Earth, no matter how rich and technologically powerful, would be able to escape the consequences of such a global catastrophe.

Chapter 7

The International Standoff

A great number of people have put a great deal of thought, concern, time, and money into investigating the possible impacts of global warming. They have created complex tools for gathering vast amounts of climate data and using this data to look into the planet's future. Their efforts have made a great many people take notice, including elected leaders and members of international organizations, such as the United Nations. These leaders and organizations are the policy makers. The responsibility for dealing with the impacts of global warming lies with them.

The Montreal Protocol

Because the problems that may arise from excess carbon dioxide emissions are global in scope, as many nations as possible need to be involved in forming solutions to them. The Montreal Protocol on Substances that Deplete the Ozone Layer of 1987 was a notable success in international cooperation. In this international agreement signed by 172 countries, industrialized nations, including the United States, agreed to phase out the manufacture of chlorofluorocarbons (CFCs) by 1996. CFCs are human-made compounds used in refrigeration products, fire extinguishers, and aerosol sprays. Developing nations, such as China and India, agreed to phase out CFC manufacture by 2006.

CFCs have been shown to create holes in the atmosphere's fragile ozone layer. The ozone layer protects people, animals, and crops from dangerous ultraviolet rays from the Sun. Even with this phasing-out, CFCs will remain in the atmosphere for the rest of the century before breaking down. Then the effects of this greenhouse gas will gradually lessen, and the holes in the ozone layer should eventually close up. The Montreal Protocol showed that the nations of the world can agree to take action when there is a clear scientific consensus on an issue, as there was on the issue of CFCs and the ozone layer.

But there is widespread disagreement on other global-warming issues. Estimates of how much Earth's temperature may rise during the twenty-first century vary widely, and so do estimates of the potential impacts of global warming. Asking the nations of the world to cooperate on solving a problem that involves so much scientific uncertainty is asking a great deal.

The Rio Earth Summit

The nations of the world took the first step toward cooperation in June 1992 at the United Nations Conference on Environment and Development in Rio de Janeiro, Brazil. Delegates from 160 nations attended this conference, which became known as the Earth Summit. They gathered in order to draft the United Nations Framework Convention on Climate Change, a document to promote agreement among nations on how to respond to the potential impacts of global warming.

The representatives agreed that human activities are responsible for global warming and that this global warming "may adversely affect natural ecosystems and humankind."[1] Despite the lack of scientific proof, global warming posed a potential worldwide threat too serious to ignore.

The Framework Convention was strictly a first step. No laws were passed. No official restrictions on carbon dioxide emissions were put into

Children greet a mascot during the 1992 United Nations Conference on Environment and Development in Rio de Janeiro.

place. The framework was more a statement of intent than anything else. It was an official statement declaring that the nations of the world were concerned about the potential impacts of global warming.

The IPCC

A year later, in 1993, the next major international group to address global warming met for the first time. This was the IPCC of the United Nations. The IPCC has continued to meet roughly once a year ever since. Many of its members, such as John Houghton and Richard Lindzen, are involved in gathering data and conducting research on global warming, but the IPCC itself does not gather data or conduct research. Instead, it assesses and evaluates the latest research on issues related to global warming for the governments of the world. The panel evaluates what this research says about the potential impacts of global climate change and about the best strategies for dealing with those potential impacts.

While the majority of IPCC members are climate scientists, the group also includes experts from such fields as economics, transportation, waste disposal, agriculture, energy, and water resources, as well as members representing environmental groups, industry, and government. Tom Karl of the NCDC says, "It's just hard to overemphasize the importance of getting scientists around the world all looking at the issue with different perspectives and different disciplines."[2]

An influential IPCC report issued in 1995 came to conclusions similar to those of the Rio Earth Summit of 1992 (see "What the Believers Say" on page 36). The IPCC report says that scientific evidence on global warming suggests that "there is a discernible human influence on the climate," which could lead to "widespread economic, social and environmental dislocation over the next century."[3]

Controversy Over an Influential Report

The 1995 IPCC report stirred up controversy because not all of the 2,500 members whose names appeared on the report actually agreed with its conclusions. The IPCC members were consulted about the issues dealt with in the report, but the document itself was written by a small committee of lead authors. The report they produced was never submitted to the full membership for approval.

Because the IPCC members were never officially polled about their opinions, it is not known how many members actually disagreed with the report's conclusion. One member who disagrees with the report, Richard Lindzen, says, "I, and the vast majority of contributors and reviewers, were never asked whether we even agreed with the small sections we commented on."[4]

Some members who disagreed with the report's conclusions accused these lead authors of deliberately ignoring their views. Dissenters such as Fred Singer and Lindzen characterized the IPCC report as a biased document. It was a political rather than a scientific document, an attempt by a few environmental advocates in a position of authority to pass off their own private views as the official views of the entire membership.

The IPCC report received extensive news coverage worldwide. Stories focused on the report's alarming findings: that climate experts from around the world foresaw worldwide problems as a result of human tampering with Earth's climate. From then on, the issue of global warming would be an ongoing one in the world press.

The Kyoto Protocol

The 1995 IPCC report helped push climate experts and political leaders to resume attempts to respond to the growing threat of global warming. The next international meeting was the Global Conference on Climate Change. This 1997 conference, which became known as the Kyoto Protocol, took up where the 1992 Rio Earth Summit had left off. For two weeks in December 1997, representatives from more than 150 nations gathered in Kyoto, Japan, to settle on a plan for reducing greenhouse-gas emissions worldwide. This plan would be an official timetable for this reduction in the form of an international treaty. Representatives would then take this treaty back to their home countries, where elected officials would vote on whether to honor it.

The treaty procedure had worked in the case of the Montreal Protocol, which phased out CFC emissions. But reducing CFC emissions had presented a relatively simple problem that elected officials could agree on easily. CFCs were used mainly in refrigerants and aerosols, limited technologies for which substitutes were readily available. Phasing them out would not create a massive problem.

But phasing out carbon dioxide emissions means cutting back on the burning of fossil fuels, and fossil fuels provide the energy to operate automobiles, to run industries, and to light, heat, and cool homes. To cut back significantly on the burning of fossil fuels would significantly impact the lives of virtually everyone living in industrialized nations.

Fossil fuels are used to provide the energy to
operate automobiles and to run industries.

To many people's surprise, the Kyoto Protocol succeeded in its initial goal. It produced a treaty calling for industrialized nations to cut greenhouse-gas emissions by an average of 5.2 percent below their 1990 levels between 2008 and 2012. It looked as though real progress in worldwide cooperation had been made.

After Kyoto

But the treaty that the Kyoto representatives brought back to their home countries was not legally binding. It still had to be ratified, or officially approved, by the elected officials of each home country. For the United States, this meant that members of Congress must vote to ratify the treaty.

There were immediate problems. The Kyoto treaty did not define the role that developing nations, such as China and India, would play. According to the treaty, only the world's industrialized nations would commit to reducing greenhouse-gas emissions. This fact prompted members of Congress to vote 95–0 against ratifying the treaty.

An international meeting was held in Bonn, Germany, in 1999 to address this crucial issue of the role of developing nations. Vice President Al Gore attended as an official U.S. representative. But neither Gore nor any other world leader could succeed in smoothing out the differences that had been steadily growing between industrialized nations and developing nations on the issue of reducing greenhouse-gas emissions. By June 2000, some developing nations had begun showing interest in playing a role in emissions reductions, but no official commitments had been made.

The Situation for Developing Nations

Industrialized nations have several alternatives they can employ to cut back on fossil-fuel consumption, including converting to nonpolluting energy sources, such as wind and solar power (see "Switch to Renewable Forms of

Energy" on page 105). And they are at work developing the sophisticate
technologies to eventually make this transition away from fossil fuels.

The situation is different for developing nations. These nations are stil
at work developing the technologies to make use of fossil fuels. Developin
nations include huge, populous nations such as China, India, and Brazil, a
well as smaller, less populous nations such as Mali in West Africa, and th
island nation of the Maldives in the Indian Ocean. The more advance
developing nations, such as China and Brazil, see themselves as being lik
the United States was in the mid- to late 1800s, when the Industria
Revolution was getting into full swing. Most U.S. citizens were still farm
ers then, living in rural areas and leading relatively simple lives, with few o
the technological luxuries, such as electricity, that citizens of industrialize
nations enjoy today.

A Different Set of Standards

What do developing nations think when industrialized nations deman
that they join them in voluntarily cutting greenhouse-gas emissions
Officials of developing nations point out that with only 1/24th of th
world's population, Americans use a quarter of the world's energy. Americ
releases far more carbon dioxide per person than any developing nation—
forty times more than India. Dr. Anil Agarwal, director of India's Cente
for Science and the Environment, says, "It is only when the United State
and Europe and Japan take the lead that the arguments about the globa
climate will have some moral weight behind them."[5]

Meanwhile, developing nations continue to burn more coal and oil t
provide low-cost energy for their expanding populations. Experts predic
that developing nations such as South Korea, Mexico, India, and Chin
will become the biggest emitters of greenhouse gases in the near future
surpassing all industrialized nations.

The Kyoto treaty will not become legally binding until at least fifty-five countries have ratified it. As of January 2001, only twenty-two nations had ratified the treaty. Half of those nations are islands, and none is a major emitter of carbon dioxide. In March 2001, U.S. President George W. Bush announced that his new administration planned to abandon the treaty entirely because developing nations were not called upon to play a role in emissions reductions.

Chapter 8

What Can Be Done?

Within the United States, the controversy over global warming became an issue in the 2000 presidential race, which was eventually won by George W. Bush. The two major candidates took opposing positions. The Democratic candidate, Al Gore, said, "There is overwhelming scientific consensus that human activity is contributing to global warming." The Republican candidate, Bush, said that, while global warming is a reality, "both the causes and the impact of this slight warming are uncertain" and that "much more extensive scientific analysis" is needed before any action can be taken[1].

Gore urged Congress to vote "yes" on the Kyoto Protocol treaty. The United States ought to take the lead by cutting down emissions regardless of what developing nations did, he said. Bush came out against the treaty because developing nations were not included. With restrictions on carbon dioxide emissions, Bush said, U.S. businesses would have to bear the cost of converting to alternate energy sources. Meanwhile, developing nations could produce factory goods more cheaply, which would cause U.S. factories to move to developing nations and American workers to lose their jobs. Gore disagreed. He insisted that Americans could save their environment and safeguard their health while keeping their economy the strongest in the world.

Dissenters React

Both the Republican and Democratic presidential candidates spoke of the impacts that cutting emissions would have on workers and businesses. Businesses that produce coal, oil, and gas feel threatened when they hear talk of cutting down on greenhouse-gas emissions. Fred Palmer, a spokesman for coal producers, expresses their deepest fears when he says that the goal of some politicians "is to ultimately eliminate all fossil fuel use in the United States."[2]

Producers of fossil fuels are not the only people who object to passing laws that call for cutting down on greenhouse-gas emissions. As we saw in "What the Dissenters Say" on page 37, a vocal minority of climate experts believes that, in the long run, global warming will do more good than harm. Their opinions on what to do—or not do—about global warming can be summed up as follows.

We do not know enough about the situation to take intelligent action. We need more information. We are very uncertain about the causes of global warming. What's more, our knowledge of the climate is extremely limited, and the climate system is unpredictable (see "Conflicting Results" on page 70 and "The Chaos Factor" on page 71). It would be irresponsible to take action now, before we really know what we're dealing with.

Global warming is a blessing, not a curse. Excess carbon dioxide should be seen as a natural way to increase plant growth, not a pollutant. Studies show that the more carbon dioxide there is in the atmosphere, the faster green plants grow, especially trees (see "Impacts on Plant Life" on page 57). And if increased carbon dioxide emissions are causing the planet to warm, then we all will benefit from the warmer weather (see "Similar Results" on page 57).

Global warming is not a serious problem. Climate experts who see global warming as a problem have an old-fashioned and wrong-headed view of the planet. They see Earth as a delicate planet that can't live with change. In fact, it's just the opposite. Patrick Michaels, professor of meteorology at the University of Virginia, sums up the dissenting view: "We are approaching a new paradigm, a new view of the world, which is going to change from fragile Earth to the concept that Earth is more resilient than we had once thought it might be."[3]

Global warming is a media event. Richard Lindzen claims that newspapers, magazines, radio, and television have created an atmosphere of hysteria about the issue, which he calls "the global-warming circus." Lindzen accuses the mass media of operating with the attitude that "any hint of environmental danger is a sufficient basis for [government] regulation unless the hint can be rigorously disproved."[4] In other words, instead of being impartial and objective, mass-media reporting about global warming is partial and subjective. Some dissenters suggest that the mass media deliberately misrepresent global warming as a dire threat to all living things in order to get audiences worked up about the issue.

The global-warming problem is a self-fulfilling prophecy. Dissenters say that something like a bandwagon effect has taken place. First a few climate experts expressed the view that global warming was a threat. Then more and more joined them. When their view became the majority view, this put peer pressure on other climate scientists to join the majority. This lead to a self-fulfilling prophecy, dissenters say. If the majority of climate experts believes that global warming is a serious problem, then it must be a serious problem.

Global warming is a dangerous illusion. Dissenters point out that while, in their opinion, the threat of global warming is nothing but an illusion, this llusion may be a threat in itself. Fear of catastrophic consequences may push governments to pass laws needlessly ordering us to reduce carbon dioxide emissions. Reducing emissions would mean converting factories, automobiles, and home-heating systems to the use of cleaner and more expensive forms of energy. And this would impact the lives of just about everyone in the nation in some way.

"It goes without saying," Lindzen writes, "that the dangers and costs of those economic and social consequences may be far greater than the original environmental danger." Like most of his fellow dissenters, Lindzen believes that, instead of government regulation, "improved technology and increased societal wealth are what allow society to deal with environmental threats most effectively."[5] In other words, they are saying that the federal government should stay out of the way and let the business community take care of the problem.

Business Leaders React

To show their opposition to federal regulation, some U.S. automakers, utility companies, and oil and coal producers formed the Global Climate Coalition (GCC) in 1989. After the 1997 Kyoto Protocol conference, the GCC issued a statement expressing its members' opposition to government-ordered emissions cutbacks, especially if developing nations were not included: "The Global Climate Coalition believes that climate change is a long-term, global issue, and therefore policies to address climate concerns must also be designed for the long term by all nations."[6] They argued that converting to alternative energy sources was impractical, disruptive, and costly.

But in the late 1990s, companies began breaking away from the GCC, including Royal Dutch/Shell, Ford, Texaco, and Arizona Public Service utilities. Here is what some of these breakaway members had to say.

"Global climate change is a serious problem and we need to take steps t deal with it."
—an Arizona utility official[7]

"We are with the future. We know we cannot go back to the old days."
—an official of an organization of 600 electrical utilities[8]

"We have to start to prepare for the orderly transition to new, renewabl forms of energy at the lowest possible economic and environmental cos while sustaining secure supplies of conventional energy as the world econ omy hopefully continues to expand."
—a Shell Oil official[9]

Meanwhile, two other business *coalitions* concerned with globa warming were formed: the International Climate Change Partnershi (ICCP) and the Business Council for Sustainable Energy (BCSE) Members include General Motors, General Electric, and Dow Chemical as well as producers of renewable energy sources. Unlike the GCC, thes coalitions accept the need for cutbacks on carbon dioxide emissions. The would rather have businesses make these cutbacks at their own rat voluntarily, but they do not rule out the use of international regulation such as the Kyoto treaty.

To make these cutbacks, these coalitions favor converting from oil an coal to cleaner-burning natural gas and renewable energy sources such a fuel cells, solar panels, and wind turbines. They insist that prices fo energy from these sources will be competitive with prices for coal and oil based energy. What's more, they argue, conversion to these cleaner energ sources is inevitable. "These changes will happen anyway," said Kirk Brown, a BCSE official. "The only issue is how quickly."[10]

Environmental Advocacy Groups React

Advocacy groups are dedicated to influencing people. They want people to see a certain issue or issues their way. Their ultimate objective is to change existing laws or to help get new laws passed that affect the issues that concern them. Western Fuels, the GCC, the ICCP, and the BCSE are advocacy groups that represent the interests of the business community in regard to global warming.

Environmental advocacy groups are also concerned with global warming. These groups are dedicated to getting carbon dioxide emissions reduced as quickly and effectively as possible. Groups such as the Environmental Defense, the Sierra Club, Greenpeace, and the World Wildlife Fund have Internet websites and run advertising and public-relations campaigns designed to educate the public and influence public opinion about global-warming issues (see "Websites" on page 122). They also organize letter-writing, telephone, and e-mail campaigns to policy makers such as business leaders and elected officials.

Strategies for Reducing Greenhouse Gases

Environmental groups, business coalitions, energy experts, and climate experts have been designing strategies for cutting down on greenhouse-gas emissions. These strategies are designed to be as cost-effective as possible—to do the greatest good for the largest number of people. Here are some examples of strategies for cutting down on greenhouse-gas emissions.

Conserve energy. The most immediate strategy for reducing greenhouse-gas emissions is using less energy. By using less energy, we burn less coal, oil, and gas. Businesses and government agencies are finding that changing the way they heat and light their offices and factories can cut emissions as well as save money in the long run. Businesses have found that energy efficiency upgrades can save them roughly $1 per square foot (2.5 sq m) of office or factory space each year. By upgrading its electric-lighting facilities, the Boeing Aircraft corporation reduced its share of carbon dioxide emissions by roughly 100,000 tons (90,700 T) per year. In a project that President Bill Clinton called the "Greening of the White House," the White House's electrical systems were redesigned to save $100,000 yearly on electric bills. "Then we put in a more energy-efficient heating system and water system," Clinton said. "Now, these are things that businesses all over America could be doing. They're things that homes all across America could be doing."[11]

Switch to natural gas. While natural gas is a fossil fuel, it is cleaner burning than coal or oil. Gas emits 40 percent less carbon dioxide than coal and 30 percent less than oil. One energy expert predicts that cleaner-burning natural gas will soon replace coal and oil as the number one energy source in America. Vehicles powered by natural gas emit 90 percent less carbon dioxide than vehicles powered by gasoline. More than 500,000 of these natural gas-powered vehicles, mostly buses, are in operation around the world.

Switch to nuclear power. About 19 percent of the electricity generated in the United States comes from nuclear power. But no nuclear plants have been built in America since the 1970s, and many of the nation's existing plants will be phased out by 2020. Nuclear power is a cleaner energy source than fossil fuels, but the American public considers its production to be too dangerous. The situation is similar in Europe

Indian Point nuclear power plant in Buchanan, New York.

Unless this public attitude in industrialized nations changes, nuclear power will play a smaller and smaller part in reducing greenhouse-gas emissions.

Practice sustainable forestry. Like oceans, forests are a carbon sink, absorbing carbon dioxide and keeping it out of the atmosphere. The more trees that are cut down without being replaced, the fewer trees remain to absorb and store carbon dioxide through photosynthesis (see "The Enhanced Greenhouse Effect" on page 29). Timber companies should practice sustainable forestry, planting many more new trees than they cut down.

Recycle waste. Methane gas, a potent greenhouse gas, rises from rotting waste in landfills to become part of the atmosphere. Recycling waste

Hybrid and Fuel-Cell Cars

Gasoline/electric hybrid cars were introduced in the United States in June 2000 by Toyota and Honda. The Toyota Prius and the Honda Insight combine a small gasoline engine with an electric motor. Both the engine and electric motor are connected to the wheels by the same transmission. Electricity is stored in batteries, which are recharged whenever the driver hits the brakes. Computer systems onboard decide when to use gasoline or electric power. This gasoline/electric combination is designed to reduce carbon dioxide emissions and improve fuel economy. The Prius and Insight are rated with efficiencies of between 48 and 68 miles per gallon (77 and 109 km per 3.8 liters) on the highway.

As of May 2001, fuel-cell cars were still in the testing stage. The NECAR 4, by DaimlerChrysler, emits water vapor instead of carbon dioxide as a waste product. This technology was first developed by NASA for use on space missions. The NECAR 4 runs on fuel-cell technology, which gets its energy from hydrogen. The hydrogen combines with oxygen to produce electricity and water, and no carbon dioxide at all. The NECAR 4 seats five people, reaches speeds of 90 miles (145 km) per hour, and can go 280 miles (450 km) between fill-ups.

Mazda and Mercedes have also developed fuel-cell test cars. U.S. car companies are expected to have fuel-cell cars on the market by 2004. Fuel-cell technology may eventually be used to power homes and factories as well.

Nissan Motor Company's first gasoline/electric hybrid car, the Tino Hybrid, goes on a test drive through the streets of central Tokyo.

nstead of dumping it in landfills reduces atmospheric methane. To further educe methane emissions, scientists are developing technologies for collecting methane gas at landfill sites. This collected methane gas could hen be used for inexpensive energy production.

Switch to renewable forms of energy. This strategy for cutting down on green-house-gas emissions receives the most attention. Many climate experts believe that renewable forms of energy, such as fuel cells, solar power, and wind power, are destined to replace fossil fuels entirely before the end of the twenty-first century.

Fuel cells, which can be used to power automobiles and buses, use hydrogen to generate electricity while emitting no carbon dioxide at all. Fuel cells work like batteries but use a constant source of fuel, usually

natural gas, to keep their charge. Al Gore predicts that the inter
combustion engines that presently power automobiles, trucks, and buses
be obsolete by the year 2020 and will be replaced by a combination of f
cells and electric batteries.

Solar power is energy collected from the Sun by solar panels, which co
vert this collected energy into electricity. Solar power is already being used
developing countries, where electric power from conventional sources ca
reach the majority of the population. In Kenya, some 150,000 families
both rural areas and cities get electricity from solar panels. The panels cha
car batteries, which in turn supply power for lights, TVs, and radios.

Wind power is energy generated by windmills. The turning of the bla
produces energy that is converted into electricity. Like solar power, wi
power has a built-in limitation that power from fossil fuels does not ha
Solar power depends on sunshine, and when there's no sunshine, no pow
is being generated. In the same way, wind power can be generated only wh
the wind is blowing. Power plants that burn coal and oil, on the other han
can operate 24 hours a day, 365 days a year.

The greatest amount of energy from solar and wind resources is availal
only at certain times of the day. So it is important to be able to store t
energy captured from these resources for later use. Storage technologies ne
to be improved. Until the technologies that use solar power, wind power, a
other forms of renewable energy are significantly improved, these ener
sources will remain secondary to fossil fuels.

Some energy experts are optimistic about renewable energy. They belie
that these technologies will be improved enough to replace fossil fu
and that the industrialized nations developing these renewabl
energy technologies will begin exporting them to developing nations. B

most energy experts doubt that this will happen anytime soon. They predict that, by the year 2020 the United States will be using 50 percent more energy than it used in the year 2000, and that developing nations will also be burning more fossil fuels. This means global warming due to human-induced carbon dioxide emissions probably will continue. If the impacts from this warming turn out to be serious, and we can't stop making the situation worse, what can we do?

Turn to geoengineering. *Geoengineering* is the modification of the environment on a large scale. The thinking behind geoengineering is this: if we have the power to damage the climate, we also have the power to repair it. If we can heat up the atmosphere, we can also cool it down. All we have to do is develop the right technologies.

Technologies are already being developed for a geoengineering technique known as carbon management. Carbon management begins by assuming that we will not cut down on greenhouse-gas emissions. Therefore, we will capture these emissions and sequester them, or store them away, deep below the surface of Earth.

Technologies are being developed for capturing carbon dioxide emissions from power plants, compressing them, transporting them to storage points, and pumping them deep below the surface. Locations for possible storage include abandoned coal mines, gas and oil wells, and ocean floors. Carbon dioxide sequestered in the ocean would be pumped toward the cold ocean floor in liquid form. On the way down, the carbon dioxide would freeze into solid chunks. These chunks would remain frozen for a long time, keeping the carbon dioxide on the ocean floor and out of the atmosphere.

Some geoengineering plans sound like they come straight out of a science-fiction movie. One such plan is to launch a series of orbiting space stations carrying vast mirrors that catch and reflect sunlight before it ca reach Earth. Plans for these space-based shields include steering system for the mirrors. By turning the mirrors at different angles, greater or lesse amounts of sunlight could be reflected back into space, thus cooling Earth atmosphere. These mirrors could also collect sunlight and beam it down t selected spots on Earth while keeping it away from others. In this way, th planet's overall temperature as well as local weather could be controlled.

Plans for space-based shields are still in the concept stage, but carbon management technologies are farther along. The Energy Departmen spent some $29 million during 2000 to study and test carbon-managemen technologies. Bill Richardson, secretary of energy during the Clinto administration, believes that these technologies could be in operation b 2010. "Carbon sequestration could offer one of the best options for reduc ing the buildup of greenhouse gases, not only in this country, but in China India, and elsewhere," Richardson said[12].

In Conclusion

The concern over global warming has grown enormously since 1896, whei Svante Arrhenius first suggested that increasing carbon dioxide emission were raising Earth's temperature (see "Early Warnings" on page 32). Fron a single Swedish chemist in 1896, global warming now has captured th attention of tens of thousands of climate experts, environmental advocates business leaders, and elected officials worldwide. It has made climate experts realize how much more they have to learn about the mysteries o Earth's climate. Global warming has some people worried that their land may soon be underwater. It has others worried that their land may soor turn to desert.

As concern has grown, so has controversy. Global warming has sparked national political debates and international treaty disputes. It has been characterized as everything from a blessing to a curse. Some experts say that global warming will bring nothing more serious than a pleasant change in the planet's climate. Others say it will bring nothing less than worldwide catastrophe. The one thing we can be sure of about the future of Earth's climate is that no one knows for sure, not even the experts.

Endnotes

Chapter 1

1. William K. Stevens, *The Change in the Weather* (New York: Delacorte Press, 1999), p. 263.

2. Alex Kirby, "Twentieth Century 'Warmest in 500 Years" (BBC News), February 16, 2000.http://news.bbc.co.uk/hi/english/sci/tech/newsid_644000/644859.stm

Chapter 3

1. National Aeronautics and Space Administration, "On the Shoulders of Giants." http://earthobservatory.nasa.gov/Library/Giants/Arrhenius

2. Peter Seidel, Invisible Walls (Amherst, N.Y.: Prometheus Books, 1998), p. 15.

3. Ibid.

4. HotEarth.net, "The Greenhouse Effect." http://environet.policy.net/warming/issue

5. William Clinton, "State of the Union address" (January 27, 2000). http://washingtonpost.com/wpsrv/politics/special/states/docs/sou00.htm

6. John Houghton, *Global Warming: The Complete Briefing* (Cambridge, England: Cambridge University Press, 1997), p.19

7. "IPCC Second Assessment Synthesis of Scientific-Technical Information Relevant to Interpreting Article 2 of the UN Framework Convention on Climate Change" (1995). http://ipcc.ch/pub/sarsyn.htm

8. *The Change in the Weather,* pp. 226–27.

9. Ross Gelbspan, *The Heat Is On* (Reading, Mass.: Addison-Wesley, 1997), p. 22.

10. Ibid, p. 77.

11. *The Change in the Weather*, Ibid, p. 271.

12. Ibid, p. 287.

13. Tamara Roleff, ed. *Global Warming: Opposing Viewpoints* (San Diego: Greenhaven Press, 1997), p. 16.

14. Fred Singer, "Global Warming: The Counterfeit Consensus," *The Intellectual Activist* (September 1997). http://www.intellectualactivist.com/tia/articles_new/singer_interview.html

15. Richard S. Lindzen, "Global Warming: The Origin and Nature of the Alleged Scientific Consensus," *Regulation: The Cato Review of Business and Government*, vol. 15, no. 2 (1992). http://www.cato.org/pubs/regulation/reg15n2g.html.

16. *The Change in the Weather*, p. 243.

17. William K. Stevens, "Global Warming: The Contrarian View" *New York Times* (February 29, 2000). http://physun.physics.mcmaster.ca/~pgs/climate.html

Chapter 4

1. *The Change in the Weather*, p. 199.

2. Jon Palferman, writer and director, "What's Up with the Weather?" (*PBS: Nova and Frontline*, April 18, 2000). http://pbs.org/wgbh/warming/index.html

3. Ibid.

4. *The Change in the Weather*, p. 177.

5. Ibid, p. 259.

6. Quinn Bender, "TV Nation," *Audubon* (May–June 2000), pp. 14–15.

7. "What's Up With the Weather?"

Chapter 5

1. "Global Warming: The Origin and Nature of the Alleged Scientific Consensus."

2. Global Warming: The Complete Briefing, p. 164.

Chapter 6

1. United States Global Change Research Program, "U.S. National Assessment: Background Information." http://www.nacc.usgcrp.gov/background.html

2. "U.S. National Assessment: Background Information."

3. *The Heat Is On*, p. 71.

4. Ibid, p. 147.

5. Ibid, p. 148.

6. *Global Warming: The Complete Briefing*, p. 157.

Chapter 7

1. *Global Warming: The Complete Briefing*, p. 175.

2. *The Change in the Weather*, pp. 163–64.

3. "IPCC Second Assessment."

4. Richard S. Lindzen, "Statement Concerning Global Warming," Senate Committee on Environment and Public Works (June 10, 1997). http://193.78.190.200/historic/files/lindzen.htm

5.   *The Heat Is On*, p. 114.

Chapter 8

1.   Sustainable Energy Coalition, "Survey Shows Presidential Candidate's Views Vary Widely on Climate Change and the Kyoto Protocol" (October 27, 1999). http://globalchange.org/infoall/campaign2000b.htm

2.   "What's Up with the Weather?"

3.   *The Heat Is On*, p. 71.

4.   "Global Warming: The Origin and Nature of the Alleged Scientific Consensus."

5.   Ilbid.

6.   "The Global Climate Coalition." http://globalclimate.org

7.   *The Heat Is On*, p. 86.

8.   Ibid, p. 125.

9.   Ibid, p. 86.

10.   Ibid, p. 96.

11.   "Leo DiCaprio, uncut," Salon.com (April 23, 2000). http://www.salon.com/politics2000/feature/2000/04/22/leo

12.   Malcolm Ritter, "Catching Greenhouse Gases." Associated Press (May 1, 2000) http://abcnews.go.com/sections/science/DailyNews/warming000501.html

Bibliography

Chapter 1

Appenzeller, Tim. "Our Fragile Climate." *Discover* (January 1994): 67–69.

National Oceanic and Atmospheric Administration. "Paleo Perspective on Global Warming" http://www.ngdc.noaa.gov: 80/paleo/globalwarming/end.html.

"Researchers Spending a Year on the Ice." *USA Today* (January 11, 1999). http://usatoday.com/weather/clisci/warctic1.htm

Tyson, Peter. "Stories in the Ice." *PBS Online and WGBH/Nova/ Frontline* (April 20, 2000). http://pbs. org/wgbh/warming/stories

"Unlocking the Climate Puzzle." *National Geographic* (May 1998): 38–71.

Chapter 2

Christianson, Gale E. *Greenhouse: The 200-Year Story of Global Warming.* New York: Walker and Company, 1999.

National Oceanic and Atmospheric Administration. "Global Warming: Frequently Asked Questions" (December 10, 1999). http://ncdc.noaa.gov/ol/climate/globalwarming.html

Pringle, Laurence. *Global Warming: Assessing the Greenhouse Threat.* New York: Arcade Publishing, 1990.

Schneider, Stephen. *Laboratory Earth.* New York: Basic Books, 1997.

Seidel, Peter. *Invisible Walls.* Amherst, N.Y.: Prometheus Books, 1998

Chapter 3

Begley, Sharon. "The Battle for Planet Earth." *Newsweek* (April 24, 2000): 50–53.

Broecker, Wallace. "Chaotic Climate." *Scientific American* (November 1995): 62–68.

Singer, Fred. "Global Warming: The Counterfeit Consensus." *The Intellectual Activist* (September 1997). http://www.intellectual activist.com/tia/articles_new/ singer_interview.html

Chapter 4

Britt, Robert. "Urban Heat Island Worsens Smog and Creates Man-Made Thunderstorms" (March 22, 1999). http://explore-zone.com/archives/99_03/22_heat_island.htm.

Karl, Thomas, Neville Nicholls, and Jonathan Gregory. "The Coming Climate." *Scientific American* (May 1997) http://sciam.com/0597issue/0597karl.html

Petit, Charles. "Polar Meltdown." *U.S. News & World Report* (February 28, 2000): 65–74.

Stevens, William K. *The Change in the Weather.* New York: Delacorte Press, 1999.

Chapter 5

Houghton, John. *Global Warming: The Complete Briefing.* Cambridge, England: Cambridge University Press, 1997.

Stevens, William K. "Computers Model World's Climate, But How Well?" *New York Times* (November 4, 1997). http://www.astro.ucla. edu/~astro7/green/climate_971104.html

Trefil, James. "Modeling Earth's Future Climate Requires Both Science and Guesswork." *Smithsonian* (November 1990): 29–37.

Trochim, William. "Introduction to Simulations"(1966). http://
trochim.human.cornell.edu/simul/introsim.htm

Chapter 6

McNulty, Steven, and John Aber. "Climate Change Impacts on
Forest Ecosystems." *Acclimations* (April 2000). http://www.nacc.
usgcrp.gov/newsletter/2000.04/Frsts.html

Miles, Edward L. "Integrated Assessment of Climate Variability,
Impacts and Policy Response in the Pacific Northwest." http://cbl
umces.edu/fogarty/usglobec/news/news9/news9.miles.html

Neumann, James, Gary Yohe, and Robert Nicholls. Sea-level
Rise & Global Climate Change. Arlington, Va.: *Pew Center on
Global Climate Change*, February 2000.

United States Global Change Research Program. "U.S. National
Assessment: Background Information." http://www.nacc.usgcrp.
gov/background.htm

Chapter 7

"Leo DiCaprio, Uncut." Salon.com (April 23, 2000)
http//salon.com/politics2000/feature/2000/04/22/leo

Lindzen, Richard S. "Statement Concerning Global Warming."
Senate Committee on Environment and Public Works (June 10,
1997). http://193.78.190.200/historic/files/lindzen.htm

Palferman, Jon, writer and director. "What's Up with the
Weather?" *PBS: Nova and Frontline* (April 18, 2000).
http://pbs.org/wgbh/warming/index.html.

"Presidential Candidates Sound Off." *Washington Post.*
http://washingtonpost.com/wp-adv/specialsales/nei/global/arti-
cle6.htm

Roleff, Tamara, ed. *Global Warming: Opposing Viewpoints.* San
Diego: Greenhaven Press, 1997.

Chapter 8

Gelbspan, Ross. *The Heat Is On.* Reading, Mass.: Addison-Wesley, 1997.

Hayden, Thomas, and Erika Check. "The Battle for Planet Earth." *Newsweek* (April 24, 2000): 50–53.

Lemonick, Michael. "How to Prevent a Meltdown." Time.com http://time.com/time/reports/earthday2000/globalwarming01.html

Ritter, Malcolm. "Catching Greenhouse Gases." Associated Press (May 1, 2000) http://abcnews.go.com/sections/science/dailynews/warming000501.html

advocacy group—a group dedicated to influencing people to see certain issues the way the group sees them

carbon—a common element that occurs in combination with other elements in plants and animals

carbon cycle—the circulation of carbon into and out of the atmosphere

carbon dioxide (CO_2)—a colorless, odorless gas present in the atmosphere; formed when a carbon-based fuel is burned

carbon sink—the capacity of oceans, coral reefs, rocks, and plants to store carbon

chaos factor—the occurence of unpredictable events within systems such as Earth's climate

chlorofluorocarbons (CFCs)—human-made compounds used in air conditioners, refrigeration products, fire extinguishers, and aerosol sprays

climate—the average pattern of weather over a long period of time

climatologist—a scientist who studies the climate

coalition—a group of organizations working together for a common cause

consensus—a general agreement

conveyor-belt mechanism—the action by which warm ocean water is carried from the tropics toward the poles and back again

developing nation—a nation in the process of changing its economy from primarily agricultural to primarily industrial

ecosystem—an environment, such as a desert or a lake, with a community of organisms that are seen as a unit

l Niño—a vast layer of abnormally warm water that sometimes appears in the ocean off the western coast of the Americas and disrupts global weather patterns

enhanced greenhouse effect—the increase in the production of atmospheric greenhouse gases by human activities, primarily the burning of fossil fuels

environmental refugees—people who have lost their homes and their means of making a living because of floods or other environmental disasters

fossil fuels—coal, oil, and natural gas formed in Earth from decaying plant and animal matter

fuel cell—a device that produces electricity from a chemical reaction between oxygen and hydrogen

general circulation models (GCMs)—computer software programs designed to simulate Earth's climate for the purpose of forecasting weather and climate

geoengineering—the large-scale modification of the environment

global warming—the increase in the overall temperature of the Earth's surface over time

greenhouse effect—the effect of carbon dioxide, water vapor, and other atmospheric gases that trap solar radiation

greenhouse gases—carbon dioxide, water vapor, and other atmospheric gases that trap solar radiation

ice ages—periods of Earth's history in which temperatures are low and much of Earth's surface is covered by glaciers

Industrial Revolution—the change from an agricultural to an industrial society that occurred in the mid-nineteenth century

industrialized nations—nations whose economies are based primarily on manufactured goods rather than on crops

infrared rays—solar radiation from the invisible part of the electromagnetic spectrum

integrated assessment models (IAMs)—computer software programs designed to assess the potential effects of climate change on the environment and on human society

interglacial period—a period of Earth's history in which temperatures are warm and little of Earth's surface is covered by glaciers

La Niña—a vast layer of abnormally cold water that sometimes appears in the ocean off the western coast of the Americas and disrupts global weather patterns

methane (CH_4)—a colorless greenhouse gas formed by the decay of organic matter

nitrous oxide (N_2O)—a colorless greenhouse gas that dulls pain in humans

ozone (O_3)—a greenhouse gas that screens out ultraviolet radiation from the Sun

paleoclimatologist—a scientist who researches Earth's past climates

photosynthesis—the process through which plants combine carbon dioxide and water to create carbohydrates

plankton—small organisms that float or drift in water

policy maker—a person in a position of authority who makes vital decisions that affect many people

proxy data—information about Earth's past climates collected from natural environmental sources, such as trees, ice, and rocks

renewable energy sources—wind, sun, water, and other energy sources that, unlike fossil fuels, cannot be used up

scenarios—possible future outcomes

simulation—the imitation of a system by a computer that is used to make predictions about how certain changes would affect the system

subsistence farmers—people who grow their own food in order to survive

urban heat island (UHI) effect —the differences in cooling and heating between the natural and human-made surfaces in a city

weather—the day-by-day changes in the atmosphere

For More Information

Websites

A great deal of information on global warming is available on the World Wide Web. You can use a search engine, such as Google, Yahoo!, Alta Vista, or Excite, to call up lists of websites. Try some of the following key words:

- global warming
- greenhouse effect
- Kyoto Protocol
- renewable energy
- El Niño
- weather satellites
- integrated assessment models
- climate

The following is a list of websites belonging to the advocacy groups and government agencies mentioned in this book. Because Internet sites are not always permanent, they may change addresses or even cease to exist over time. The sites that follow have been in existence for quite some time.

Environmental Advocacy Groups

Environmental Defense Foundation
http://www.edf.org

Sierra Club
http://www.sierraclub.org

Greenpeace
http://www.greenpeace.org

World Wildlife Fund
http://www.wwf.org

Business-Based Coalitions

Western Fuels Association
http://westernfuels.org

Global Climate Coalition
http://globalclimate.org

International Climate Change Partnership
http://iccp.net

Business Council for Sustainable Energy
http://bcse.org

U.S. Government Agencies

National Oceanic and Atmospheric Association
http://www.noaa.gov

National Climatic Data Center
http://www.ncdc.noaa.gov

National Aeronautics and Space Administration
http://www.nasa.gov

National Environmental Satellite, Data, and Information Service
http://www.nesdis.noaa.gov

Environmental Protection Agency
http://epa.gov

International Agencies

Intergovernmental Panel on Climate Change
http://www.ipcc.ch

United Nations Environmental Program
http://www.unep.org

Index

Page numbers in *italics* are illustrations.

About the Author

Ron Fridell has been writing since his college days at Northwestern University, where he earned a master's degree in radio, tv, and film. He has written for radio, TV, newspapers, and textbooks. His other books for Franklin Watts include *Amphibians in Danger: A Worldwide Warning, Solving Crimes: Pioneers of Forensic Science, and DNA Fingerprinting: The Ultimate Identity.* He taught English as a second language while a member of the Peace Corps in Bangkok, Thailand. He lives in Evanston, Illinois, with his wife Patricia and their dog, an Australian shepherd named Madeline.